PRAISE FOR *CLEARLY N*

A hypnotic, surreal, and lyrical testament to the capacities of friendship and the outer limits of love. The enigmatic Serala will be impossible to shake from your consciousness.

MARGAUX FRAGOSO, AUTHOR OF *Tiger, Tiger*

In electric, adventurous prose, Eli Hastings tells the story of loving one wrecked soul, and the rich, dark wonder of the joys to be found along the way.

PAUL LISICKY, AUTHOR OF *The Burning House*

An unflinching account of how it feels to be young and flirting with the abyss in America and an investigation into the dangerously different ways that people respond to addiction.

RACHEL ROSE, AUTHOR OF *Giving My Body to Science*

Clearly Now, the Rain is a wonderfully seamless story that orbits around a young man's passion for a tragic young woman. But no matter how strong the devotion, no matter how intense the commitment, this memoir is a disturbing confirmation of how the power of addiction all too often overwhelms even the greatest love. Hastings writes from the heart, with unnerving honesty, and a remarkable sense of compassion.

JAMES BROWN, AUTHOR OF *The Los Angeles Diaries* and *This River*

Clearly Now, the Rain

ELI HASTINGS

A MEMOIR OF LOVE AND OTHER TRIPS

ECW

Published by ECW Press
2120 Queen Street East, Suite 200, Toronto, Ontario, Canada M4E 1E2
416-694-3348 / info@ecwpress.com

LIBRARY AND ARCHIVES CANADA CATALOGUING IN PUBLICATION

Hastings, Eli, 1977–
Clearly now, the rain : a memoir of love and other trips / Eli Hastings.

ISBN 978-1-77041-077-0
ALSO ISSUED AS: 978-1-77090-292-3 (PDF); 978-1-77090-293-0 (EPUB)

1. Hastings, Eli, 1977–. 2. Hastings, Eli, 1977– —Friends and associates. 3. Hastings, Eli, 1977– —Travel. 4. Friendship. I. Title.

CT275.H28725A3 2013   973.92092   C2012-907513-2

Editor for the press: Michael Holmes
Cover design: Bill Douglas
Typesetting and production: Carolyn McNeillie
Printing: Edwards Brothers Malloy   1   2   3   4   5

PRINTED AND BOUND IN THE UNITED STATES

For her, of course. And for the rest of us.

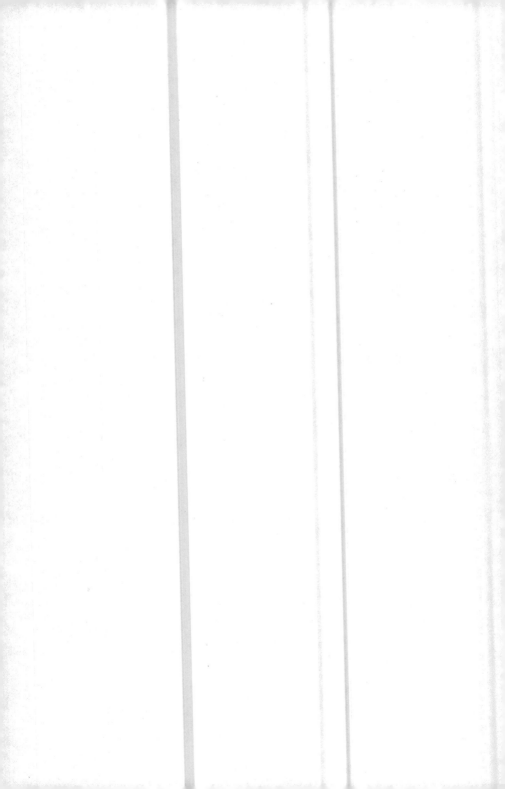

Prologue

MY TRUCK IS STALLED IN the middle of a skinny one-way street in the University District. Rain slides down the windshield and distorts the gray world outside. My fingers are wrapped around the steering wheel, knives and clubs on the floorboards. Hugh is as taut as a stretched bungee cord at my side. The ripping of traffic in the rain comes from Forty-fifth. Luke answers his phone in the backseat. *Get out guys,* he says. *Get out of the car.* And there are so many things, so many possible pieces rolling up from the back of my mind, and we're out of the truck and Hugh is shaking, more scared than I've ever seen him, and my hands can't hold the keys so I put them away. Luke clutches a raspberry smoothie with one hand, holds the cell to his head with the other, marching back and forth in front of the truck, listening, waiting, for what we don't know because he won't look at us, won't answer the broken whisper every few seconds. *What's going on? Who is it?* And the rain comes down harder, the mist gets thicker, and commuters stare at us as if we are ghosts.

Part 1

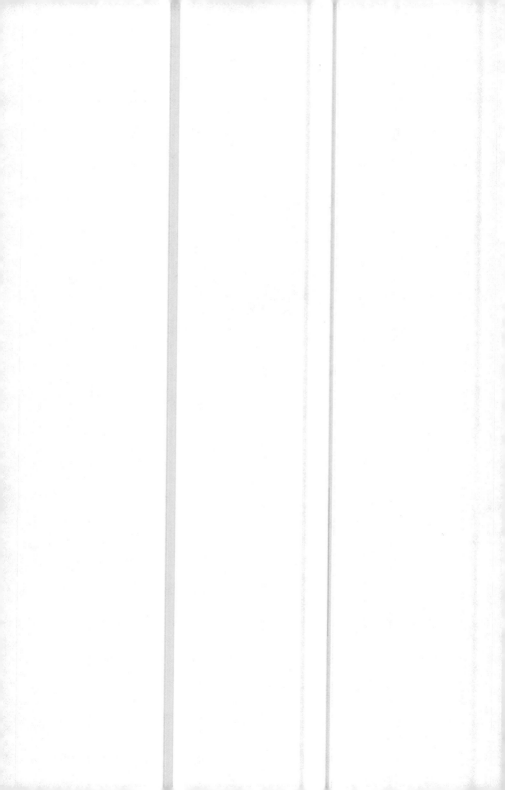

One

WE'D BEEN FIRED INTO AMERICA like pinballs. We were joyous young clichés, Louis and I, with our jointly owned VW van, Kerouac stories, and bags of drugs. We'd only become close in the last year and we were a strange pair: Louis near six feet, broad shoulders, black hair shorn mostly off then; I was short, skinny, blond hair growing into impossible tangles which, to my eternal mortification, I'd later try to pass off as dreadlocks. He carried the love of many people because of the high school years of designated driving, generosity, the shoulder he offered for adolescent crises. In short, he was full of humor and kindness and I was intense, rather self-absorbed and embittered. But we sensed the space our friendship had to grow into and the will to *go* was something we shared in that spring of 1996.

There were a lot of elements that went into my momentum away from Seattle then. Only two months after we tossed our tasseled caps, Louis and I had moved into a newly constructed, spacious five-bedroom with three other high school friends, courtesy of a crooked realtor who demanded cash and no rental contract. The scenario was, at first, the culmination of a dream we'd all shared for years: no more classes, no more books, no more busywork and what passed for education at our inner city high school. We all got service sector jobs and pooled our money for discount groceries and beer, believing giddily for a time that we were crafting an adult community from the ranks we all considered as close as family. But the dreams of high school die hard and the mismatched workaday schedules, the filth multiplied by five adolescent males, and the pressures of bills came together with considerable speed—as fast as we'd alienated our entire residential block with parties and late night dramas on the back porch.

One January night Louis and I lounged in his back bedroom, the drapes pulled against the nastiness of the winter; I recall waterlogged leaves splatting against the pane in the wind like wet rags. A drunk stranger weaved past Louis's open door, presumably looking for the bathroom. I shoved it closed and turned Bob Marley up on the stereo, sliding a glance at Louis who, for the first time I could recall, was scowling along with me. In the soupy light of the candles and the far-away optimism of the reggae, we both silently discovered in that moment that this communal party life was not what we'd dreamed. It was no kind of destination and, at least for now, in the middle of that dead, freezing post-high school season, Seattle had become a husk and we had to empty our bank accounts and try a more extreme version of freedom: a road trip with no destination.

I'd also left behind a disturbed friend. There had been a fissure running through him for years, and in the last months it had finally yawned wide, becoming full-fledged schizophrenia. This development brutally erased any hope I'd harbored of helping him. Getting physically distant was a partial balm to my guilt, disappointment and fear, conjured forth by a very rough ride at his side.

My brief experience with corporate America, as an espresso jerk in the financial district, was another element that caused me to walk away from my familiar life with a straight spine. They had rules, which now seem a reasonable part of customer service but then caused me great consternation: you had to "strike up chat!" with and smile at every single customer who came through the door. That little shop hosted some angry and sad moments: when they 86'd the Professor, a sweet and silent homeless man who voluntarily swept our sidewalks, because a banker complained about his smell. It was not a context in which I fit and the impulse to untie the apron and fling it down in protest grew acute quickly.

My most vivid memory from that job is the phone call: I was in the midst of the mid-afternoon rush, whirling from the espresso machine to the garbage can with a steel tub of scalding coffee grounds in hand when the phone rang. The apple-faced manager said with bright annoyance that it was for me (we weren't supposed to receive social calls at work, needless to say). I dumped the grounds, absorbed the pointed sighs of the waiting businessmen, hooked the phone under my chin and learned that one of my best friends, Hugh, had just lost his big brother—a role model to us all—to suicide in his parents' home.

These were some of the events that sent me off bitterly into America, to be as naïve and recklessly free as possible until college began in the fall. I believed I deserved it, as if it were my only chance, as if I weren't on the track to a private liberal arts school and a life of sampling experience, of the luxury to explore.

With these blinders on, with this momentum, I traveled toward Serala for the first time.

ONE OF MY AND LOUIS's first stops was Sage Hill, the small college we would enter six months later. Our friend Jay had already started there, straight out of our ghetto high school. By the time Louis and I made it down to visit that corner of Riverside county, beneath the brown air and hard sunlight of the desert, Jay was already deeply in love with Serala.

Jay wasn't the type to flip easily over a girl. I'd known him since the seventh grade when he'd a been an intellectual band geek, his passion and authority on many subjects so grown-up that it used to dumb most adolescents into silence—those whom it didn't grew comfortable in Jay's orbit. In the eighth grade we'd been urged into an extracurricular debate class together and I'd come to appreciate Jay, and to see that his bombast—always impressive, not always welcome—arose from insecurity. One thing he'd always had, though, was a funky and intimate relationship with rhythm, and he graced the high school jazz band, and, in college, both punk rock and hip hop crews with leadman presence. He had thinned and refined into an oddly handsome and sophisticated cat by the time he met Serala.

Man, I don't know how to tell you, I'm really trippin' over this girl, he'd reported to me late nights on his dorm phone that winter, blowing smoke out in frustration. *There's no way for me to say what it is she does to me. She's hard but so good—like drugs almost. But she loves different.*

THE FIRST TIME I SAW her, I was scared of her. I wonder if it showed.

She is sitting in the corner of a cinderblock dorm room. She smokes furiously—not fast, but with drags that seem lethal. She is silent and her eyes are purple, bagged, like they've weathered a storm. Her south Indian skin is as dark as her pupils. She watches us severely. I try to tell myself that she is clearly a hamper on the good times we've planned with Jay, and that I don't give a shit what she thinks. But these falsities evaporate every time I feel her aloof gaze hit me.

Soon the silver dollar sun is halfway dropped, shadows are growing and someone has produced malt liquor. We are in a dorm room next to Jay's that has been abandoned in typical private college fashion: the administration has not even noticed that spoiled teenagers are turning it into a den of vice. Someone scrawls a quote on the wall and I follow the lead. I rise with drunken steadiness in the dying sunlight that leaks in from the window over Serala's shoulder, and slash a large RIP for Hugh's brother across the east wall. I tell myself I'm eulogizing my dead classmate, but I'm also thinking that this might gain me Serala's attention. And it works: within moments, she touches me for the first time—gives up her drawn pose on the desk chair, eases near and puts a cool palm on my neck. She tells me with that touch that I am allowed in. I feel my good fortune open in my chest.

DURING THOSE DAYS THAT LOUIS and I lingered at Sage Hill I remember her picking up every expense and warning off our protests with glares. Jay was walking on clouds. I suspect she could have gotten him to drive her to Tijuana for an ice cream cone if she desired, but she wasn't like the game master girls of high school, collecting favors, gifts, and affection for sport. She didn't seem to be asking anyone for anything—except sometimes to leave her alone for a bit.

Jay would speak of her urgently, always shaking his head as he did so, as if he only half-understood this person and what she was doing to him. He could be honest about this with me because he had years of trust and comfort to draw on; in her presence he was more outwardly confident and more aggressively charming than ever.

She drives me fuckin' nuts, man, he'd say, and sometimes I could glimpse the fear alongside the love, the thin line that ran through his heart. A preview of storms to come.

There is one picture of her that rises above the blur: in the institutional laundry room of the dormitory, white cinderblocks and white washing machines and her, sitting halfway inside one of the dryers, where someone had tossed her, skinny limbs spidering out, dark as a shadow sweeping the desert against all that white. She's giving the camera a look of pure defiance, daring the viewer to chuckle, restraining her own laughter, as if this tomfoolery were serious business, her middle finger raised.

WHEN WE GOT RESTLESS, LOUIS and I climbed into the VW van and hit it.

We stood beneath the thousand-foot walls of Zion National Park; we rolled through its snaking byways, beating drums on the dash to Marley and De La Soul. We completed ill-advised scrambles around the Grand Canyon. We made it to the smack-dab center of America, where we lodged ourselves with an old filmmaker and weathered a Kansas twister. Then it was south, to the heavy-aired magic of New Orleans and the madness of Jazz Fest. Then further, to Georgia, where we abused the wealth and generosity of my relatives, borrowing BMWs and pushing them down freeways with the fire of good whisky. We hiked in the magic light of the Smokies. We rambled to Providence where we lived with wild artists and the days filled with basketball games on sticky courts deep into the spring. In West Philly we got lost and came face-to-face with local thugs who decided to let us pass with only cold glares and the flash of a pistol. Then to Boston, in and out of close and not-so-close friends' lives, gobbling up hospitality as quickly as the ounces of weed we'd mailed ahead of ourselves.

Jay had found his way to a plane ticket to join us for a spell, motoring the East Coast. It wasn't till we scooped him at Hartford International that we learned we were expected at Serala's house that night—before Serala herself would fly in from L.A. twenty-four hours later.

I recall nearly swallowing my tongue at her mother's beauty. The confident way she swings her green eyes around is so similar to her daughter but without the edge. She piles us into the leather interior of her Lexus and takes us to feast at McDonald's.

The next morning her mother drives us into New York City and, en route, does no less than the following: smokes skinny cigarettes, drinks coffee, converses with us, opens and closes files on her laptop, cuts off several drivers, talks on her cell phone, and yells at a traffic cop who, in her estimation, is doing a poor job. Us Seattle boys clutch door handles and do our best to impress her with our wit and intellect, both dampened by the driving experience and a great deal of weed.

In all the years that came after, me sitting shotgun beside Serala, I never mentioned the driving traits she'd inherited; I just fastened my seatbelt and smiled. But I did consider that having a mother with that much poise and bearing must have prescribed her a durable veneer, right from the beginning.

And so Serala arrives that evening, looking poorly rested and nervous at the fact of home. That night we slouch around a booth in a diner. Jay is doing what Jay does when he wants to impress: monopolizing the floor, talking and talking to demonstrate his knowledge of sundry subjects. Louis is doing what Louis does well, too: nodding Jay along, laughing, inserting jokes, helping him carry the burn of the limelight.

But I don't mind just watching Serala smoke and drink coffee and Coke, alternating sips. Once in a while, when my eyes are on the ribbons of taillights outside the window, I feel her gaze land on me. When she leans over to her friend Cassie with a long ash on her cigarette and mischief in her eyes, and whispers in her ear, I strain to hear but cannot except for the effusions that they want us to hear, the flirty, showboat phrases suddenly shouted (we were still teenagers after all): *no way! I did* not *say that! Fuck you, you're one to talk. Cassie, you better not—shut up!* Later, walking down a street near her house, Serala wordlessly takes my hand in hers and holds it tight until we get to our destination: a lit-up court where we play drunken tennis with our hands.

AFTER THAT LOUIS AND I made another huge loop in the center of America and, cruising a Colorado highway with a bottle of honey wine one July day, we decided to drive home. After three months, some twenty-six states, seventeen thousand miles, and countless adventures and mishaps, all that was left was one more ribbon of highway. I had gained more than what the wild sociology of the American road had afforded me; I had gained the caliber of friend that would be by my side in many unforeseeable journeys down the line. Louis carried his love like his bass guitar—slung easily and comfortably over his shoulder, less forgotten then grown into. While I'd spit all my hurt and rage about my parents and stepparents, about my crazy ex-best friend, about Hugh's brother, about ex-girlfriends, Louis nodded, slapped my shoulder, rolled another joint, switched the tape.

When I see Serala again in the parking lot of Jay's place in Seattle in mid-August, I find her face altered, and not merely by the hoop through her lip. The usually flawless skin beneath her eyes is raw and her lip quivers. I've learned that Jay slipped up and cheated on her and, now, this has left her unmade for the stage of the world. She slides a tissue-wrapped knuckle across her cheekbones. It leaps off my tongue:

I'm sorry about what happened; I think it's fucked up.

I feel awkward, standing there, trembling a little in my flip-flops and ragged shorts. But when she pitches her Pall Mall, blows out the last plume, stands and looks me in the eyes, kisses my cheek and wraps skinny arms around me, I feel like I would kill for her.

Thanks, I can really use that, she says against my shoulder, and her voice warbles from shaky to firm, the timbre of both the hurt girl I want to soothe and the tough screw I already admire. Maybe this is also the first time I really notice the sculpture of her jaw, the curve of her long neck, the near-perfection of her chest (or, as she would say, *how great her tits are*). The first time I inhale deeply of her perfume, the expensive musk that lurks in shirtsleeves and linens, and sometimes, it seems, rides in on a sudden breeze.

I am flying down to school the next day for some reason, so I watch them all pull away, Louis and Jay in our van, Serala in her Honda Accord, which she'd named *Desert Storm*. A caravan of youth, vanishing.

AT THE TIME, THE GIDDINESS I felt about Serala was conflated with the giddiness I felt about college, departure, a blank page, an unblemished space in the world and I wasn't given to analyzing it too much. The truth is I didn't like myself too much. I was hungry for childhood to be decisively done because the events of my life didn't fit under the thin skin of a kid anymore. In truth they had not for a long time, beginning with the ugliness of my parents' divorce, which was knotted up in my father's abuse of drugs, alcohol and other affairs, the revelations of which turned my childhood into a kind of false floor in my memory. But in recent years the casual way that violence and betrayals and sorrow cropped up had increased in velocity: the mental illness of my best friend, the suicide of Hugh's popular brother, the betrayal by a girl that I'd loved wildly. From beneath a baseball cap with a keg cup in my hand, devoid of wisdom or perspective, I flailed. The best I could achieve was catharsis by risking my ass writing graffiti on rain-soaked billboards or dropping acid and playing chicken with freight trains. I wanted to deal with life's pain better and I thought that college and all its attendant lessons would instruct me in how to face storms like a man instead of a boy.

Likewise I can say now that Serala was the human manifestation of that. I knew that she had endured rougher trials than me.

I saw in her a stoic and mature model, a contrast to my adolescent hunt for catharsis and circular ranting in Louis's ear. I wanted to grow up intentionally as opposed to being costumed in adulthood by events and feeling absurd in the cut of those clothes. I wanted to be perceived like Serala and, like Serala, respected.

I had no idea what the toll was for that kind of a journey.

Two

MINUTES AFTER OUR ARRIVAL AT Sage Hill College, this time as students, Louis and I sit on "the mounds"—little hills with fake grass—and listen to the president's welcome speech. She is a large woman who smiles too much to be believed. She is wearing a sweat suit. It is one hundred and fourteen degrees.

I'm dressed comfortably because this is a free-flowing community, she explains, making grandiose gestures with flabby arms.

Louis and I scoot into the shade of a transplanted tree and talk genuinely about fleeing—back to any of the places we found ourselves the season before. But when I glance at my friend—my road partner—his big, sunburned face tilted to the side, trying to make sense of the nonsense they're feeding us from the podium, and I see everything I feel reflected in him, I am equally ready to continue forward. So when the poisoned sunset spreads, when we start to smell weed and hear music, we haul boxes from the van and build high school shrines with tape and curling photos on the cinderblock walls of our dorm rooms.

Although Louis and I are not roommates, he's just down the hall. A gangly, pale kid who will be my roommate wears a look as if he's been blindsided by this relative adulthood. When I drop my jeans and cut the quarter pound of Seattle green off my thigh, I think he might faint. But he recovers.

As the party gears up on our hallway that night, the same hallway on which I met Serala months ago, I hear snippets of chatter: *Hey, dude, do you skate?* / *No, bro, I don't know what it means, I just thought it would be a cool tattoo* / *I'm totally gonna take the easiest classes, man.* My anxiety about higher learning begins to drain away but disappointment laces through me, too—it sounds like high school out there. And I have a hard time imagining Serala in this bastion of image and ease, even as I witness her here.

TRYING TO BALANCE LOVE AND concern, Jay betrayed her for the second time that fall by reading her journal. I might have done the same. The ferocity with which she said it to him: *It's my fucking business, don't—just don't.* A mark that might sneak from beneath a sleeve or a bra strap, the acid that would run through his veins as he tried not to ask, tried to believe the half-truths and denials.

So the second time Jay reads her journal, she puts an end to their relationship.

He calls me in desperation one afternoon and I go to him. I find him in his room, the drapes drawn tight, Miles Davis's *Kind of Blue* rocking the stereo. Jay's collapsed on the floor, tears and butts and straying splashes of Jack Daniel's mixing in the ashtray in his lap. The wreckage that I'd anticipated is in the foreground.

All of Jay's bright presentation has inverted into a disaster of mucus and tears, all of his plumage knotted in disarray. He uses his fists on raw eyes that won't stop.

And I would see Serala then, too, on one of her midnight campus rambles, the slow way she'd look up when I ran into her, the sleepy smile in the sleepless night. I'd see her vanish from a smoky crowd and return far calmer. I sit down on the ratty carpet and can see her at that very moment, even as Jay cries softly and the clock tower does its five o'clock song: strolling angrily off to her car, or placidly into her dorm, depending on which side of the score she is on.

There is nothing to say to Jay in those moments—I had already learned that much, ironically, from Serala, about wasted words and the moments when language would fail.

I can't do it, he says, between slugs off the bottle, *I can't fucking pull myself up by my bootstraps this time.* His broad brow and thick lips are contorted. I join him for a drink and start assembling ad hoc wisdom in my head. But he continues. *She's with that motherfucker right now, I know. That motherfucker came in here the other day calling himself my friend and told me he that he wouldn't do this to me—came of his own free fucking will.*

Jay hits the bottle, harder than he has yet. The moderate light of an autumn evening comes in muted by curtains and the stir of shadows grows in the corners. I hate Serala then. And it isn't only because she is hurting my friend. It is mostly because I think that she can, and so eventually will, turn her back, that she might not be the person I've been casting her as—and that I don't want to consider.

Samar: I first saw her high in a tree, dancing wildly above a party of a thousand undergraduates. Her legs secured her on a bough, muscular suggestions under a red skirt, dreadlocks whipping against the polluted sky. A security guard pulled her down from her perch and I followed her into the night. She stayed late in my room, chaste but taunting with her eyes, and borrowed a knife with which to walk back to her dorm. She came from a childhood in the meat grinder of Beirut, escaping through Mediterranean islands with her mother, eventually to an upper-middle-class existence in Massachusetts. I was ridiculously smitten; she rose like a phoenix as all the girls of my adolescence turned to ash in my head. Samar was a survivor but not a victim, roughened but not incapacitated by the wrongs of her world. She gave me a place to put all the bitterness that crowded in me. The militancy with which she spoke against imperialism, the indignation that she wielded after seeing powerless people cut down as a child—it tapped directly into my anger, which I still couldn't explain to myself. Even when she tried to image herself as a fasco-feminist, tried to be masculine, gruff, drinking heavy beer, belching and refusing to shave her legs, her sex appeal made me stupid with desire. I lied to myself, I resisted, and I talked my drunken way into other girls' beds. But when Samar put it to me, smoking cigarettes one October day under the brutal sun, *Should we just say we're seeing each other until we say something else?* I rushed in with my heart bared.

Maybe two days after that, Samar and I are finishing a frustrating, passionate tussle in my bed (she is postponing sex for some cryptic reason). The dark is finally complete outside the glass and the sounds of life and party slip under the door: popcorn popping, TVs blaring, the Beastie Boys thumping along. I light a cigarette and see her profile in the brief orange glow.

She kisses me again and says, *I'll be back later—I'm going on the hunt for weed.*

Later didn't come before sleep, and later didn't come before dawn. Later came at the end of the next day, when she called me down to the quad and took a deep breath and told me she'd been with Jay. I slammed two doors. And then I went to Serala.

OUR FIRST MEAL ALONE IN California: Denny's on an offshoot of Route 66. A hot Sunday afternoon in late October 1996. She has Coke and coffee and fries; I'm forking some kind of nasty omelet. We discuss poetry, especially the Beats. We discuss Jay, Samar, Serala's new man, Monty, and the emotional incest of our little college. She adds a big breath of carcinogen to the restaurant's stratosphere and cuts her gaze at me. I swallow omelet quickly.

What?

She narrows her eyes and leans closer to me. I didn't know at the time why I saw the flicker of fear along with the hesitation. But her voice shakes when she says, *Eli, I want to let you in.* Then she takes a drag because her throat has caught and surprised her. *I carry so much around.*

I have the sense to nod attentively and steal a French fry.

It's not that I need help, you know, and she looks over my shoulder and takes another drag. *It's just that I think I want you to know me.*

I nod again, but that isn't cutting it.

I want to know you, I add stupidly, but it's true. After a moment of staring, just a hint of vulnerability in her face, she changes the subject.

We climb into her Honda, the absurdly named Desert Storm, and crank the windows down, open the sun roof, light Pall Malls, turn on the radio, and drive like mad, like we are tackling the American road, like we won't stop till Mexico, like this is all we need—even though there are really only three miles between us and campus.

As we pass through the last stoplight she starts fiddling with the radio. She tusks Pall Mall smoke through her nose in frustration at the lack of good choices, her jeweled wrist and fingers close enough to my leg to make me nervous. She finds the opening bars of "I Can See Clearly Now," and she twists the volume and turns her opaque shades on me and shows her perfect teeth and we say, both at once, *I love this song!*

ONE NIGHT IN LATE NOVEMBER, when California has finally given up the ghost of summer, Serala comes to visit my room. Late at night, more often than not, my room was candle-lit, Pearl Jam songs floating out of the speakers, windows open for the Santa Ana gusts. It is her birthday—and Louis's too, incidentally. She has been celebrating by eating very strong ecstasy. She's like mercury, or quicksilver, like the loops of jewelry she will, in later years, take from her neck and wrists each night and pour from one hand to the next like water. I can barely get her properly seated on the bed. She tips sideways and forwards, drops her lit cigarette, giggling and *oopsying!* It's as if only love and innocence remain in her. It's like the first times I got stoned: the hilarity overpowering, the uproarious, childish jokes. Her face is contorted and illuminated with laughter, eyes running, mouth wide, a loss of control that burns through her awareness every few seconds and causes her to clamp a jeweled hand over her face. But then something else gets us going and she is gorgeously wrecked all over again, so far from her cage.

She staggers to the stereo and starts pressing buttons. *Dylan, I want to hear Dylan, I want to hear Dylan!* She's like a toddler, demanding her way. I try to explain we'll have to load a Dylan disc, but she isn't hearing it, just trying to work magic with her clumsy fingers, her face lit neon blue from the digital readout, pieces of ash floating free from her cigarette.

Hours later I lay sleepless in my sheets, smiling at the image of her smiling, eyes heavy lidded, half-toppled over, giggling. For her birthday I gave her a stainless steel ashtray, wrapped in purple paper. It gained me a slurry exclamation of joy: *Yay! I love presents!* And that childlike grin breaking again and again around her white teeth.

That was one of two times that she admitted to being happy.

Spring break, 1997, I traveled to the San Joaquin Valley to volunteer for the United Farm Workers' Union. After a week of labor, the call came that my father had fallen eighty feet from a cliff in Costa Rica.

He had been struggling out from underneath the darkness of two failed marriages, a soon-to-be empty nest, and the evil Seattle weather. But really it was severe depression that had sent him off to a foreign land to search. He had been a strong and fair father, an excellent friend to many, a sly but just businessman, and a deeply flawed husband and chooser of mates. He'd struggled with cocaine, alcohol, women, and his weight, but what it all boiled down to was the noose of biochemistry that lay just barely slack around his neck. Those of us who were closest to him—me, my brother Luke, and a couple of friends—had seen his departure for Central America as the first decisive and courageous step he had taken away from the quicksand of his life.

In the Seattle hospital he was Life-Flighted to, the hospital that killed him twice with negligence before resuscitating him, where I had to sweep desks clean of their contents to get the attention of a nurse, my brother and I hardened. Luke had been an imaginary-friend-collecting type of kid, in no small part because such disconnection kept him insulated from the ugliness of two divorces. But over the course of his first adolescent years, he'd morphed into a confident, popular, charming young man. He was, in fact, at the time of dad's fall, living in Barcelona becoming bilingual, experienced in sex and drugs, and absurdly cosmopolitan for fifteen years of age. But he still deferred to me as his big brother, was still my tentative admirer—yet ready for my rote verbal abuse. And he still bore the burden of jester for our family, even in this darkest chapter. His narrow face and chaotic dirty blond hair, his light blue eyes attentively darting—it's all still framed vividly against a background of nurses and tubes and bladders of saline solution. Luke was ready, like a hair trigger, to try to make Dad laugh or, just the same, to join me in the hospital's stairwells to pound steel doors until bruises appeared on our fists.

With angry tenacity on his part, and against all prognoses, my dad survived—shattered and agonized and addicted to narcotics, but walking.

I returned to Sage Hill for the last few weeks of that semester and Serala was the only one who didn't make me feel like a

Martian. She did better: she made me feel like everyone else was a Martian. Coming from the savage battle for my father back to a place where people's concerns were as superficial as which beer to buy, or as academic as an armed conflict thousands of miles away, closed me into a very lonely space. I was bitter on behalf of my father, and no one could grasp that—in fact it wasn't permitted. I was supposed to be happy.

While sitting with Serala on the mounds under an orange tree one night, slugging a bottle of wine, the sky richened by a bad day of pollution, I report my dad's precarious climb back into his life.

It's, like, people keep saying to him, whenever he mentions the pain he's in or the struggle to get by, "Oh, you should be so happy you're alive—it's a miracle, you know!"

I'm about to explain further, to say that my dad is sick to death of hearing that shit. That he is grateful to be alive but that's not enough to get him up into his suit of agony each day. But Serala doesn't need me to say more. She makes a face as if the wine were suddenly bad.

God, that's awful. He must be fucking sick of hearing that claptrap—what a selfish thing to say to somebody who's suffering. It's shocking, Eli, sometimes even to me, how people always make things easier on themselves, even when they see someone they love hurting.

She shakes her head and lights a smoke. I wouldn't have been able to identify my father's friends' behavior as selfish, I would have dubbed it a simple lack of understanding, but Serala is right—it is selfishness, however unconscious.

We spent a lot of time reclining on the mounds, smoking, watching the poison in the sky. We laughed and snuck hits off a pipe; we watched people and talked trash, innocuous cruelty that made me feel better—like punching a wall, but without injury.

But even in our mutual solace, by May you could have packed the bags under her eyes. When I pressed, she allowed that sleep was a sweet and distant thing to her.

THE SHARPEST STRIKE OF TRAUMA in my life at that point was my father's fall. Standing over him as he was far away in a coma, gripping his hand in the ICU, watching machines breathe for him, made every parcel of fear and hurt I'd come up against before pale in comparison. But I learned I could wage battles with poor odds in the adult world and win—that Pyrrhic victory was a bitter gift I treasured. I also learned a lot about other people and their incapacity to engage with the terror I'd missed six weeks of school to stare in the face. Friends that I fully expected to be at my side as solidly as they had been at house parties were simply at a loss, and newer friends from Sage Hill became acutely uncomfortable around me because their lives were finally the party they'd been looking forward to back in their rigid private high schools, under the thumb of conservative parents.

Even for those who were courageous enough and cared enough to want to be there for me, the imperative to explain my experience with my father's mortality and then his suffering was exhausting; it was all I could do to catch up on schoolwork and keep my temper before the vapidity of social and academic concerns. Serala ratified everything that I'd dared to hope for from her at this time—it wasn't merely that she understood; it was that I didn't even have to explain. She developed my own thoughts, as if she could see they needed help evolving. She gave me the permission to percolate with unlikely but very real rage when people embraced me and exclaimed, "I'm so happy your dad's okay!" She offered me membership in an inner circle that I hadn't known existed and of which she was the only full-fledged member I'd met.

But it was more than that. I finally had something to offer her, too, if only because I'd been through a nightmare. She began to trust me as a place where she could be free and open, where her levity would be safe, where it wouldn't ruin her to drop her veils—as on her birthday when she came to me with the joy of a child. It didn't occur to me then how sad it was that only a hundred dollars of chemistry could produce such a trick. I didn't see any of this then. I simply thrilled at the intangible love blooming like a planet between us.

Three

BY THAT SUMMER, SAMAR HAD found her way back into my life, determined to put her betrayal behind us. She and Louis and I started descending the coast from Seattle in late August, having filled the van with all of our belongings now that we were sure we'd stay at Sage Hill for three more years. We stopped in Portland for a Taj Mahal show at the Rose Garden. It was an awkward event with Oregon yuppies and obnoxious rich kids (I still didn't place myself in this same pigeonhole) and I was glad when it was done—we had what now felt like a new life to get back to in Riverside.

As we double-time it up a hill, I remember how I parked the van kind of crookedly, and I hope that no zealous meter maid has ticketed me. We round the bend and three breaths catch. It's gone.

Later the cops will find our beloved van, set of so many wheeled, teenage dreams, emptied of all our possessions and broken down. Later, we will get well paid by my mother's homeowner's policy. Months later, on a San Francisco street, Samar will see a girl wearing what she swears is her hat, and we'll follow her for a dark block or two, at a loss for what to say or do, until she vanishes into the night.

IN MY MEMORY IT IS September 1997 when the sails snapped up and college moved forward in a lurch. Classes started and El Niño hit: days, weeks of impossible water flooded the town. Walking anywhere meant soaking yourself to the knees. Two kids died when a sycamore fell on their car; you needed an eight-cylinder vehicle to power through the worst of it—and that, at least, Louis and I had. We had squandered our insurance money on a 1965, drop-top, sky-blue, Buick Skylark. The car was the sparkling center of our lives, and any let-up in the tempest was excuse to roar around town, pretending we were rock stars.

Serala was fading into a realm occupied only by Monty and a small circle of others. What these characters shared, mainly, was a streak of caustic humor and cynicism about the do-gooder school they'd wound up in. At least that's all I thought they shared; there was also the question of drugs and money.

I walk into the common room of her suite one Friday. The sounds of college recreation float around outside: a missed Frisbee clattering on cement, skateboards rolling, Peter Tosh crooning to "Legalize It," laughter and shouts. Serala is dressed in her customary black, thrown over a sofa like a discarded coat. On the chairs and sofas around her, three members of this clique whom I don't know recline in similar poses.

Hey, I say, *what are you doing?* In the time it takes her to swing her eyes up to me and focus, we could have had a short conversation.

Livin' it up, she says, finally, and a broad grin sneaks onto her lovely face. Her apparent detachment allows me to look her over. Usually meeting her eyes is tough. The strange thing is that she looks so good: smooth, taut skin, sculpted jaw, a thin and graceful neck, collarbones rising from her chest like wishes. Her perfect teeth and storm of jet-black hair, freed from her usual tight ponytails and buns.

What's happening this evening? I ask, just making awkward conversation because I am in of a room of zombies. She shrugs, lying there on her back, so the motion is like opening her chest to me. She gives that grin again and reaches for a smoke, but misses the pack. I dig one out and light it for her. Around me the kids scarcely stir; their gazes are on the small square of sky out the window or the flaking ceiling. As if they're watching TV.

I don't know how to feel, and the cleaving of my mind is the type that would occur many times in the future: there she is, possessed by poisons, playing with her life, destroying her insides. On the other hand, there she is: safe, comfortable, for the moment not feeling any pain.

I COULD TELL IN THOSE days that the honeymoon was over for Serala and Monty and she was in the grip of a hard love—just like me. When I finally had Samar and settled in, I began to punish her. I had buried most of the pain that I'd suffered from her casual betrayal with Jay. I treated her as if she had the abuse coming and it was my prerogative to mete it out as I felt proper. But I was improper and I was cold.

I find myself one night pissing in the bushes in front of a house where a party thumps along in the backyard. As I zip up and turn, I can see Samar chatting with this tall dude a few yards away. There is the briefest measure of time that I can see myself mutating, going back to the same insecure, vindictive boy I was in high school, but then I have ice water in my veins. I watch her laugh at something, throw her head back. I return to the keg to keep fueling. When she approaches me with a smile, I turn my back on her.

What the fuck?

Get away from me, I say, as severely as I can. She holds her ground. Samar is not a girl to surrender any ground. Samar spent much of her early life being mistreated by males. From her abusive, corrupt father in Beirut to the string of New England lovers who welcomed her with manipulation and deception into the game of love, American-style. She has every reason to expect this kind of shit from me, but she hasn't.

I saw you with that fucker—I shrug in his direction and spill beer over my hand—*so why don't you go back to him, huh?*

You're trippin', she tells me calmly and flatly, leaning forward into my face to say it. Then she walks away.

Mercifully, I don't recall how it all turned out. I know I went as far as to call her a slut, to insult her clothing as trashy, to leave her at that party out of spite and drive home. I was a mess, I was a child, and I was taking out more on her than could be justified by the most liberal rationalizations. I acted as Serala's inverse, flailing to her calm, vindictive to her forgiving. Meanwhile, she'd tell me of Monty's philandering with a near-whisper, as if it was something *she* was ashamed of.

Two memories rendered in the infrequent sunshine of that season:

Samar is idling in a friend's dorm room at Messert Hall when through the window she sees Serala approaching. She mistrusts Serala as much as Serala does her and she lifts her chin and looks away. She expects a glare at worst, so when Serala lights a Pall Mall and knocks on the glass to call her outside, I imagine Samar is taken aback. When Samar gets there and Serala says, *I don't give a shit what you think about me or if you like me or not,* I imagine Samar recovers her composure, and sees an opening. Serala says, *You hurt my friend and I hope you don't do it again.* I imagine that the gravelly roll of skateboard wheels from the quad devours the brief silence. I imagine that Samar says something back, like *yes, okay, you've got every reason to dislike me. I won't hurt him again,* uncrossing her strong arms. And I imagine Serala says, *good,* and blows smoke past her and then says, *I guess what I mean is I'm giving you a chance, I don't want to hate you, I just want him safe.* And she drops her butt and crushes it and forces a smile and then puts her gaze on her feet—in that way she has—and walks away.

The second:

It is a weekday and Serala and I escape for a meal, both of us fed up with our unhealthy love affairs. This time we do better than Denny's—St. Charles, a café with high booths and a Cajun theme. We drink beers at midday; I remember sitting outside, the sun a welcome sensation after long, wet days.

We are doing writing exercises, something that our odd, beloved creative writing professor has pushed on us like a flu shot. The scritch-scratch of her blue pen gets urgent. Her brow is furrowed and locks of hair are hanging down over it, escaping the big sunglasses that hold most of the bangs to the top of her head. She bites her lip once, hard, I can tell, because a ridge of caramel flesh is white from the dent of her teeth. Then she pauses and curses in a way that is supposed to be sardonic but I know is actually somewhere nearer to happy.

Fuckin' A. She holds up the leaf of notebook paper by the corner and lets the breeze rattle it. *This is what we got, Eli. This is it.* She shakes the paper. *Painters have these big heavy canvases, texture, and color. Musicians have pounds of material hanging from them and they beat their art right out into the world with it and watch how it affects people, right there! Right fucking in front of them.* She wags her head and slaps the paper down, reaches for a smoke. *All we've got are these flimsy fuckin' pieces of paper, weightless. They'll fly away quiet, fast, and easy. We got it rough.*

We climb back into Desert Storm. We light cigarettes and tear down Route 66 with guitar banging on the radio and we smile because we find that fleeting intermission of freedom again before the reality of Sage Hill swallows us. As we round the last turn she fiddles with the radio. I feel like the idea got into my head a fraction of a second before the tune did: "I Can See Clearly Now," just starting up. We look at each other and smile and don't need to say a thing.

THOSE LAST SOGGY WEEKS OF 1997 felt more cramped, mainly because we were bound for Study Abroad programs in the spring. I hugged Serala goodbye on the bleached concrete outside Messert Hall and we agreed to come together through words. We were to meet for lunch dates where we would both write letters at mid-afternoon—once she settled into her Parisian sidewalk cafés and once I settled into my Venezuelan watering holes.

(HERE IS MY PARENTHETICAL NOD to chronology because I learned it right here in time; here's what she told me on a tiny postcard that read *Christmas Love*; here's the bad stuff; here's the savagery of my duty; here's the consequence of her moments of peace in that drug; here is when I began to guess at the horror she'd endured. What I mean is, here's the shape and shadow of it, which is all that I have to offer, because it's all she's offered me: in Riverside, at the end of the term, there is a man and his hypodermic blessing, there is her frail form rendered helpless by it, there is the advantage he takes with his lust and his fists, the two confused and conflated; but there is the oblivion of her sharp mind, the detachment of her old soul and on that postcard, which I read in front of the mailbox with adrenaline swirling through me, she shrugs it off—*not so bad,* she claims. And more: in Connecticut, just before she flies away, slides a black ocean between herself and home, there is another man, one she used to know who tries to but cannot hurt her, because despite warm flesh, a distant pulse, a sip of air, despite his knife gleefully lacerating her in private places, it seems that her grace remains untroubled, because, again she claims, *she is not really there.*)

Four

BEFORE I KNEW IT, I was shopping Seattle's awful February streets for bug spray, sunscreen, and an inauspicious backpack. I was saying goodbye to Samar over long, dramatic telephone hours.

The closest I came to capturing Venezuela was in those imaginary café lunches that Serala and I convened for: her scribbling with frozen fingers in a French street, me sweating in a humid Venezuelan noon, the pages that then drifted slowly, back and forth over the Atlantic.

Mérida was high in the Andes in a valley formed by craggy peaks. If you dared the suicide switchbacks to reach such altitudes, they would take all the warmth from your bones, render your alpaca hat and sweater silly with one driven gust. When we first arrived, all my wrong expectations went the way of spindrifts I would see smoking off blades of mountains. Venezuelans were supposed to be hospitable and open. What the "preparatory reading packet" didn't mention was that Mérida was an anomaly; it bore more resemblance both in climate and character to cold

European places. Packed buses were often silent and upon greeting a stranger you were as likely to get an indifferent stare as a nod.

I walked down those streets and pedestrians avoided my eyes. I moved into a Catholic house and three generations of women who lived there treated me with kind formality. I went to sleep at night (by plowing through fat cans of Polar, the national beer) after failing to get a familiar voice on the sketchy phone lines.

ONE AFTERNOON, AFTER LUNCH, I push through the wrought iron front gate to return to the city center. I catch sight of the bus at the stoplight, affectionately dubbed the "Gray Buffalo" by its driver. The cylinders of two-dozen dirty vehicles growl and huff. I pull myself aboard and dump myself onto the last seat in the back.

Soft lamentations, directed at no one in particular, come from sticky vinyl seats, *Ay, Dios mio, este calor . . . insoportable sol, coño . . .*

Indeed, it is a freak weather pattern that brings this heat suddenly blazing. There are many children: over a dozen of the blue-shirted, pleat-skirted schoolkids on their way back to class after lunch. Two black girls with sweet voices play a singing game behind me. Through the window I see a blade of a woman in a white linen dress bargaining hard for a block of cheese and a barefoot child trying to catch an older one on a bicycle.

I put my attention on the *Harper's* article I'm reading, a scathing review of Angola, the Louisiana State Penitentiary. Among other abuses, prisoners are often coerced to participate in the annual rodeo, which usually wraps up with maiming and even deaths.

The slowing of the Gray Buffalo, and the rustle of bodies, tears me from the article. An adolescent mestiza is suddenly leaning over me to peer out the window, the scent of her humid flesh in my nostrils, her black curls swing cool against my cheek. From the front of the bus, whispered prayers and exclamations unfold, seat by seat. The cause of our delay appears outside my window. A man has been run down. He is dead—or else seconds from it. His head is mostly severed and he has literally been knocked out of his shoes. He is fairly young. His face holds a contorted expression that could be delighted surprise. The driver stands curbside next to his damaged car. He crosses his arms and rocks a little on his heels; he nibbles a cuticle. He holds an awkward smile on his face, a look of profound embarrassment.

When the horror registers, I turn away like waking from a nightmare. The cleavage of the mestiza is still pressed against me as she cranes her neck to catch the longest glimpse possible. I can hear her pulse.

All of the children are clambering around, squirming between appendages. They are transfixed, like they might be at a magician's trickery or a cartoon. The older people shake their heads and grimace. The crowd reorganizes itself, "Ave Marias" and other benedictions rising from the seats, the motion of the sign of the cross.

I go back to the article. The story is well written but inconclusive; a Justice Department investigation is pending at Angola.

When we reach downtown, I enter the current of midday and find myself on shaky legs. I quiver under the eave of a bar. A breeze brings a scrap of newspaper to rest against my leg, a headline and most of an article: *LA VIOLENCIA SURGE (VIOLENCE RISES)*. Instead of my errands, I find myself in a dark corner of the bar, pouring Polar beer through my nerves.

THIS IS SOME OF WHAT I learn in her letters from the Old World, a composite of the spring of 1998:

Big, soft DJ headphones cover and warm her ears; sweet, sad music that makes her a little bit more okay pumps softly through them. A long wool jacket wraps her torso and she loosens it a bit as she goes, pulling up the hood—the better to slink through the throngs of men with hungry eyes. She's been too proud to betray any fear, but on the inside the violence of their stares has cut at her and she wants someone on some mornings, someone it's okay to be scared with, to hold her tenderly, someone to dab away her quiet tears with a steady hand. But now she is all right; she is walking, twilight a silvery promise on the horizon. For a while she puts her eyes on the ground as she walks, in that way she has, just the same as pulling up her hood—to take her a little bit further from the bandstand of the world. *This old Paris is okay,* she thinks, the wine and the coffee mixing in her veins, her face pleasantly cold against all the warmth under her jacket. When she emerges from the narrow streets of an unfamiliar neighborhood, she suddenly knows exactly where she is: beside the Seine, a block from Shakespeare and Company, crossing the bridge to the busier side of the city. The way the brown river is flowing—*dirty but fucking pretty* she thinks—it calls her to pause on the bridge. One of her favorites is coming through the headphones now, either "Drunken Angel" or "Jackson," maybe. And as she lights a Pall Mall, and the drizzle picks up, and the two waters mingle, their clarity and their dirt, as waiters hustle to crowd chairs under umbrellas, as the booksellers bang closed their kiosks for the night, and it all seems to happen in time with Lucinda Williams, Serala thinks that maybe, just maybe, this might be enough. And she's shocked to see the swollen lip of the sun peek out for a moment before day is done, but not as shocked as she is to find herself standing there in the rain smiling at it.

THE NIGHT SEEMS THICKER THAN when she entered the bar. She removes her shades with reluctance, remembering Allen Ginsberg's warning: *It is uncool to wear sunglasses at night, unless, of course, you should be wearing sunglasses at night, in which case, you know, it is uncool to take them off.* The stir of shadows around the bus stop seems heavier. Gin burns in her, roiling the gastric juices in her stomach, which has shrunken into a negative space since the last time she choked down a meal with her aloof host mother. The bus is half-empty and she lurches aboard, grabs a pole, and steps away from the man who already stabs her with his eyes. She puts her shades back on, faces away, but he sidles up, says something lewd in French that she can't make out. *Fuck you*, she tells him and he laughs like a gunshot and grabs between her legs, hard, chattering on, something about brown girls. And then he knows what's happened before Serala does, reeling from her jab, his lip hanging raggedly open, blinking stupidly, dripping blood on the expensive shoes of commuters. Her hand hurts but she doesn't care and she stumbles off the bus onto a corner where a café spills generous light. And at her back she knows that strangers witness her as scrappy and tough, that heads in the bus window turn with respect for her. And she's pleased in a way, of course, but it doesn't change the fact that now she wants to cry and be held as anyone, weaker or stronger, would. But there is no one for this and instead she's off at a trot down another ancient street, searching for the black door where she will find what she needs. Where she will find the thing that can do the trick that gin cannot, will ease the aches in her spine, will let her sleep maybe even until tomorrow, will make her feel better than held, better than loved, better than rested—even if she has to go away from herself for a while to get it.

ONE AFTERNOON IN MÉRIDA I sat at a sidewalk café that resembled a French café—one could order café au lait and wine, though I stuck with hard coffee and beer. There was an old waiter who chain-smoked, and well-dressed citizens with newspapers; umbrellas were placed to shield us from the mountains' sudden storms. It was that day I wrote a line I recall clearly, seared into my memory by its flagrant naïveté. It went like this, in response to Serala's self-destructive revelations from Paris: *I would love you no matter what, even if you told me you were going to take all your pills and go play on some French freeway.*

I WENT AWAY FOR SEVEN weeks to the northern Caribbean coast, leaving behind most of the telephone and postal service. She hit the rails of Europe with her friend Cassie and had a blast, recalling the *I wonders* and the *maybes* and the *ifs*. In the end it seemed like maybe France was a wash: a lot of unhealthiness, trouble from piggish men, and a lot of loneliness, but also proof of strength, some moments of possibility. The lesson: she *did* miss—and *did* have—the love of many good people oceans away.

I like to imagine it as a single moment:

She sits at a sidewalk café. A smattering of strangers populates the tables, everyone arranged so that everyone else has the maximum of space around them, all angled toward the finale of a bright spring day. Serala has her sunglasses and her cigarette smoke and her woolen coat with the floppy collar, so she feels cozy, hidden even in plain sight. A French version of Camus's *The Stranger* lies open next to her diary, which holds waterfalls of her blue letters. As the tangerine light grows richer, she loosens her scarf and she's suddenly hit by an image of me, facing the same horizon and dreaming of our reunion, and she almost smiles thinking of how many long meals and poems and road trips we have yet to share. She feels excited even, ready to return. And as her cigarette burns down and the day starts fading like it's on a dimmer switch, the faces of all the people that she loves spin through her head. And the remaining bar of sun goes out like a wick in pooling wax, she stubs out the smoke and, for the first time in her life, a few tears arrive without pain.

WHEN I PICTURE THE TOWHEADED boy, just barely clear of teenagedom, dressed in a weak attempt at Mérida's formality, hunched over a tiny circular café table, filling his veins with caffeine and beer as liquid midwives to his words, I chuckle. The melodrama of my and Serala's "imaginary lunches" is sweet and nostalgic—the fetish of poetry and romance of handwritten pages, wielded like weapons or lightning rods. But I'm glad of that overly earnest kid, that terrible writer, not only because my commitment to Serala caused me to record my experience and make it real to myself, but because it fused us closer. I didn't know when I made the vow to meet her on the page that it was the only way I'd really know her; at the time it was consolation for not being in her presence for many long months. I know now that if I hadn't sent her my fuzzy truths, I would not have received her stark ones and might never have had another chance to prove I was brave enough to hear.

I had a burning need for her to hear me and understand me as I bumbled through that other world like a drunk alien. This need isolated the other lessons just enough that I could absorb them. For one, I was receiving the lesson of solitude. I had no one in Mérida aside from my straight-backed Catholic household and three female Sage Hill students I saw infrequently; no one spoke English and no one was going out of their way to incorporate some blond yanqui into the brilliant weave of that culture, as I had hoped and dreamed among my pre-journey jitters. My life had always been attended by a best friend, a girlfriend, or both—not to mention a broad social circle. The lonesomeness of the first weeks was terrifying in itself. The fact of being strange in addition to solo brought me to tears at night in the shadow of an avocado tree; I wanted to snap the neck of our rooster myself when he sang down the day at dawn and announced another cycle of heartsickness. But because I had to articulate this to Serala, I had to wait for her response. And so I had to hear her gentle admonitions to suck it the fuck up and embrace the challenge of anonymity and silence, which eventually taught me more than any person has.

I didn't know then why the violent death of that pedestrian was the loneliest moment of the semester, but I do now: I had just seen a body for the first time, a grotesquely destroyed body at that. Everyone around me had reacted with meager curiosity. I, on the other hand, had been hypnotized for only the briefest moment—and then horrified by my own interest. My life—with a handful of exceptions—had been sheltered from violence. The flurry of punches I'd received and given, the infrequent streak of bloody bodies in a house party or the slashed face of a drunk on the streets of Seattle composed my limited kaleidoscope of experience. That's truly what it means to be "first world": insular. I was alone in a universe so hard-knock, so raw, that grisly death caused only a soft stir—how could I not feel like an alien?

Likewise I only know now why Serala flew into my mind that afternoon, why it was her that I wrote a letter to with a trembling hand in a downtown bar: she was the loneliest person I knew, because she saw things distinctly from others. And perhaps she saw things that others did not, as I felt I had—the twisted pleasure in the dying man's face, the appalling amusement in the driver's.

Not only that, though—it was also that Serala didn't share my privileged cocoon of insularity, that violence both by choice and by the whirl and stab of fate's hand was not foreign to her like it was to me. She had witnessed violence as an EMT volunteer on the fast roads of New England—lodged in my brain are her tales of scraping motorcyclists off the asphalt, or cutting leather from a spine-damaged man who would later threaten to sue over his ruined jacket. I know these traumas sometimes excited her; I can see her dark eyes alive on the shoulder of the turnpike, reflecting the spinning red of sirens. I can see her, working around a shattered body, perhaps altered by adrenaline or something more. I know that she experienced violence at the hands of others, though she always refused me the specifics. I know that she even inflicted violence from time to time when she was scared enough.

When I tried to talk about it—both the sight of the dead man himself and the nightmares that came later—my host mother would wave her slender hands in a cancelling motion, rub at the crucifix on her neck. My fellow students would rotate their faces sharply away from my words like birds. Though Samar and my father were sympathetic, the buzz of the interminable phone line brought me no tangible empathy. Serala was unreachable except by the pen but I had the assurance that when the words fell, she could catch them, and that made all the difference.

Five

THAT SUMMER MY DAD STRETCHED his strained credit—to say nothing of his destroyed body—and took my brother and me and our ten-year-old Lab, Sky, to the borderlands of Minnesota. We spent a week portaging and rowing through countless lakes with Dad's old friends, catching walleye and roasting them on campfires. My dad was determined and strong, plodding up steep slopes with his cane, fatigue and pride alternating on his face. Evenings, Luke and I would take a canoe and circle whatever little island we'd planted ourselves on for the night. Ostensibly we were fishing, but mainly it was a chance to smoke joints, practice Spanish, and talk about Dad.

Luke's sinewy arm whips back with the rod and I dodge the yellow lure, nearly dropping the joint.

Cuidado! Shithead.

Luke gives me a stoned giggle by way of apology. The lure plinks into the mirror of black water thirty yards away and he leans against the middle bar in the canoe, reaches back for the joint. We both gaze toward shore where Dad is trying to navigate a steep slope at the bottom of which Sky's bright blue racquetball bobs in the water. Sky stares at the ball and back at my dad in the same way she looks at the walleye coming out of the fire. Dad missteps and slides on his right heel a couple of feet, then gets his cane planted and rights himself, shockingly.

Whoa! Luke exclaims, like we're watching a sporting event.

Dad, presumably stilling his heart, pauses before the main event of bending over to retrieve the ball and casts his eyes out to us. He's wondering if we saw. I wave; Luke throws a thumbs-up. Dad wags his cane, apparently proud of not falling rather than pissed at himself about slipping.

You think that Dad got what he was looking for?

The question blindsides me.

You mean even though he smashed himself to bits?

I intend the question to be sardonic, but as it comes I realize it's genuine, this notion. Luke nods, swings the lure, toting a length of lake slime into the canoe. He turns and faces me over the tackle, wrestling with a blue spinner.

I don't know, dude. But I'll tell you this much—he's probably way too stubborn to ever give up now that he's fought this hard.

Luke bobs his head and smiles. I don't tell him that there have been times when I did very much think Dad was going to give up.

Plink, splash. The racquetball hits the water and Sky is en route. Luke's blue spinner is a dazzling arc in the afternoon sun. Dad waves again when he sees me looking, just leaning on his cane watching his sons—afloat.

ON THE ROAD HOME WE stop at Glacier National Park. While my father and brother and Sky goof around under a roaring waterfall, I sit on a rock and let the Montana sun spread a burn on my shoulders. I can listen to the near voices of my dad and Luke, the pound of the water on rock. Far below a gust of wind clears the throat of a canyon. The lowing of a boat in the lake rises up. But these are sounds that are more like silence—just a backdrop.

Serala had once seen this country, had known it more intimately than she would have wished: the cobalt blue water, the mountains scooped out, as if by a celestial spoon. Her folks had sent her off, one winter, to the reformatory power of Outward Bound, a survival course meant to knock the trouble out of kids. It was because of her forays into drugs that she was sent (though I doubt her family knew the extent of those forays). She'd fought through it like a champ, blowing off the two-pack a day habit, not to mention the drugs—as did the other torn-up teenagers around her, deprived of other options besides reform school or Juvie. She bent stoically to those weeks in the altitudes where, five people to a tent, one had to be cranking out sit-ups to transfer warmth to the others—all night long.

I was wired on hope that summer. I reclined on that Montana rock, fresh from ten days of watching my father refuse the straightjacket of disability and live, when only a year before he had plummeted nine stories and been expected to die at countless moments. I was just months departed from my ultimately successful journey to Venezuela where I'd survived alienhood, learned Spanish, and even come to love solitude. Likewise I carried a stack of Serala's letters from the Old World in my worn JanSport pack, wrinkled pages of blue ink that contained a renewal of determination between the lines. If I'd held back some with her in the past it was because loving her frightened me; while her friendship and loyalty were incalculably valuable, the liability of losing her to the darkness of addiction and its attendant hazards was comparably huge. But I read enough resilience into her letters—perhaps because I wanted to—that I believed she, too, was renewed and would return, like me, stronger. My own narcotics were hope and faith, born of my father's triumph over death and disability, Serala's triumph over all the darkness that had tried to drown her over the years, my own triumph over insecurity and lonesomeness in Venezuela. I was inebriated on this brightness on that flat rock in Glacier National Park while all my blessings shimmered around me like the diamonds of water floating free of the waterfall and catching the sun. I even decided to move in with Samar in September—it felt as if everything in the world could work out.

I LOVE THAT COCKSURE TWENTY-YEAR-OLD, but mostly I envy him. I'm glad I didn't yet know a thing about the flawed biochemistry of my own brain, which would slam a cage down over my entire world in a few months' time. I'm glad I didn't know what was coming for my father: little pink pills and a blooming death wish. I'm glad I didn't know about the origins of Serala's struggle then either.

Despite glimpses, the magnitude of her trauma and the force of her ghosts were still clothed in vagaries. I could fathom the abstractions of "abuse" and "addiction"; I could even guess at how rough it must have been for her to wrestle with the fallout of those things in the context of a traditional Indian family. If I'd known then the depth of her pain, I might not have allowed the libations of hope to swoon my head that summer.

I learned it all much later—the broad brushstrokes, anyway, something about the events that had gotten her shipped to Montana years before. And I took those brushstrokes and I filled in the rest for myself, inevitably and probably wrongly:

She's sixteen, doing the suburban teen summer thing in Connecticut—serving sandwiches to sunburned mall goers. She has been bound in the loose standards of Grateful Dead music, sundresses, overalls and the East Coast's bad weed. But the angst that defaces most adolescents has erupted in her. She's turned toward the darker allure of Nirvana, the nihilism, the world-damning cynicism—toward this mini-culture of my own home, Seattle, where at that age I am happily oblivious with my hip-hop, classic rock, and cheap beer. There's an older girl that she works with, a tall, severe beauty who slaps bread and cold cuts together and squeezes mustard bottles with a dull violence. This girl plays with her nose ring and stares into the distance, or sneaks out for cigarettes when the manager goes on break. She makes Serala nervous; Serala admires her. When the older girl speaks to her, Serala does her best to sound worldly, caustic, and older. When this young woman watches Serala change into her banana yellow apron out of a Nirvana T-shirt one day, she nonchalantly invites her to a party. Serala keeps her cool, shrugs, and tosses her hair, casually agrees. But secretly she's overjoyed and hoping that she'll get a stronger taste of this glimpsed world. She's already admitted to a couple of friends that she wants to try heroin, that she imagines herself adult enough to dabble and suck the pleasure carefully from the experience.

At the party there is the wailing and bleats of some grunge band or another ripping the speakers, people lounging with half-lidded eyes or chopping powder, loosing those maniacal cocaine laughs. Serala sits in a corner, smokes, and tries to look unconcerned. When the man sidles up and offers her a taste, she's suddenly scared, her theatrics are faltering. A metallic taste climbs her throat as she looks at the coolly disguised urgency in his face, the distance in his glassy eyes. But she glimpses her coworker studying her from across the room. Plus, the allure of the forbidden tugs in her belly and she says, *yeah, sure, why not,* and allows him to lead her into a bedroom lit by a bulb with towels nailed over the windows.

Her pulse is racing as he cooks up a spoonful, talking nonstop to her, quiet and kindly, promising that *she will love it, that she'll never be the same,* that it is, for him, *the best part of life.* When he turns her skinny arm under the bulb and pinches at a vein, perhaps she tries to pull away, perhaps she's flooded with flight juice, perhaps she begins to argue or plead, a child suddenly frightened by a bully's tricky game. Or perhaps not.

I imagine that first time, when the spike that will bind her bites and the rush comes through her like a transfusion from an angel, that her head falls back into the pillow that the empty space in the room has suddenly become. I imagine that it's so good that even as he pulls her clothes from her, she enjoys the sensation of air moving over her skin, that she's unaware that he's no longer cool, no longer slow and careful but fast, somewhat angry, and that his hands are closed around her arms. I imagine—perhaps because I want to—that she is absent and free. I imagine that the horror and the shame only break like the dawn does, well after the facts are in. I imagine that by the time she is home, running the shower to get it hot, to wash off the filth of that vanished man, she sees her eyes in the fogging mirror and finds nothing but a deep silence in them. Because she's discovered something terrible: she can endure what has just happened—and not even make a sound.

Six

BACK AT SAGE HILL IN September, in the ascetic basement dorm
room Serala has christened the Batcave, we sit and smoke, sifting
through her notes from Europe. A blear has ruined the sky, I
am nursing a tequila hangover, and she is quieter than usual. I'm
vaguely frightened of the things she might tell me about France;
I've ascertained that the relative cheer and optimism I read
between the lines of her letters rotted and fell away nearly as soon
as she returned stateside—certainly by the time we returned to
Riverside. The worst thing was not Monty's repeated cheating
while she was away, but it wounded her more than I might have
guessed.

Read this, she says, *this is how I feel.*

> *he looked at her through hunger,*
> *and her white silk slipped off,*
> *pooling on the ground*
> *like spilled milk.*

I was honored to be allowed to see the human, scorned-lover kind of pain that was antithetical to her act.

Well, I think you've nailed down how it feels, I say carefully. I mean I know how it felt when I got cheated on. He's a fucker, you know?

He could have done worse, you know. A pull off a Pall Mall, blown through her bedroom window. *Everyone slips—don't I know it.* A long pause and her eyes turn to a far corner. *I can't shop for gems when I've got no cash, you know?*

ON A GLOOMY OCTOBER EVENING at an outside table at St. Charles Café, I ask Serala if the poetry she's writing helps her spirit, if she feels more human laying it down. She says *no*, sharp as a rifle crack, and I say, *That's bullshit.* She has a drag of smoke in her lungs. She turns bloodshot, unslept eyes on me that ask: *How dare you—who do you think you are?* The waiter grabs a dish and turns away and she says, bittersweetly, *Fuck you, Eli Hastings,* and I smile and she fights her smile, but loses.

There were so many times when one of us stopped on the edge of the unsaid and we were synched enough to know the rest of the sentence—maybe that was good enough. A nod and a swallow of wine, the gaze breaking away only with effort, but still a table between us, still tables of strangers to rein us in. I remember looking away those moments, at the peak of one of our exchanges, and catching a half dozen pairs of strangers' eyes before they could turn away, back to pork chops and salads and gumbo.

So I'll say now all the things that I didn't say explicitly then, to make damn sure it's not only Serala's dirty laundry that's hung across these pages: with the autumn came the inverse of all the healthy, hard-won faith of the summer. I was driving some nights with eight kids in the Buick, the top down, on Route 66 and off again to the side streets, a fifth of tequila in my body, racing other blacked-out men, no idea where the car was in the morning. My father was hurtling downward again too, brushing death, risking his life and others' everyday, driving through the narcotic fuzz of OxyContin self-righteously, because he wasn't sure he cared anymore. And I was learning of the futility of changing others when I couldn't even answer the dark questions boiling in me. Because there were times I got so sad without knowing why that it whispered over into rage and I found myself in the kitchen with a knife against my hand, amid smashed dishes and overturned furniture in Samar's cookie-cutter apartment. There were times in those months when I let the sick giddiness—like going up on psychedelics—ride its way through my mind and I could picture me and my convertible arching against the sunset, dropping hundreds of feet down an Angeles canyon to an end that fit my inexplicable fury.

On an April night in 1999 the Santa Ana winds are coming across the hot land like kind spirits. It is a mundane Friday evening: I find myself at a house party where we're packed in like a suitcase of elbows. Because of events of freshman year, Samar considers the host of this party, Alicia, to be her nemesis. That night, feeling careless or perhaps destructive, I toss off my hesitation and chat with Alicia as long as I please—even after I see Samar come through the door with stupefaction which quickly turns toward murder in her eyes.

With enough beer, and my back to the kitchen where Samar has vanished, I manage to really forget her, and to enjoy catching up with Alicia. When I enter the bathroom, I pause to check myself out in the mirror before pissing, which is damn lucky because Samar crashes through the door and lands blows on my head and chest before I wrestle her out. A good third of the party has gone awkward for what they've witnessed when Samar comes stomping back through.

Somehow I feel calm—enough to piss, wash my hands, look at my eyes in the mirror again. In Samar's wake, people give me glares or shake their heads in sympathy, depending on their allegiance. Outside, she is sitting on a rock in the garden, hands clutched over her head. She speaks before I can.

Fuck you. It's over, fuck you. Tugging at her dreadlocks.

Samar, why don't you try to calm down.

You asshole—fuck you, it's over. She will not look up; people are clearing away.

Samar, you don't get to take this back tomorrow. I realize, only as it comes out, that I mean it.

It's over. She almost whispers.

It's not violent, even a little soft. And I know it's true, just as well as I know that she won't want it to be in the morning. And I finish my bottle, point myself toward Serala's dorm—some two miles north—look at down at my feet, and start walking.

IN THE COMMON ROOM OF her "suite"—as they euphemistically called them—a good-hearted drunk from Zimbabwe and my friend Marshall are drinking forty-ounce bottles of Olde English and watching *Cops*. I slump down next to them, just feet shy of her bedroom door.

Marsh, is there still an empty bedroom at your house?

Yup.

Can I move in tomorrow?

Word.

Thanks.

He hands me the forty and I take a swallow, knock knuckles half-heartedly, and lurch toward Serala's door, knocking with my forehead.

Given all the things that might have been transpiring at 3 A.M. in the Batcave, I should be glad I only interrupt wine, hash, and Portishead. But I'm not thinking that then; I'm thinking— strangely, as her eyes find me, and then in silence she puts her arms around me, and Monty kindly steps out, and I begin to weep—that I am home.

As the door clicks behind him, we are left in the penumbra of a desk lamp with a scarf thrown over it. As that first round of tears runs out, I feel sheepish. When I lower my hand from my eyes and turn around, Serala has opened her bed, folded the covers back. Her stuffed parrot is on the pillows, waiting to comfort me, and so is she: sitting on the bared space of the futon, knees drawn up, ashing her Pall Mall onto her jeans and rubbing it away with a finger. She catches my eye with a look that is knowing and comforting, her jaw slack and still; she knows exactly what the ledger of damage reads.

She pats the futon and I undress mechanically, then climb in and attempt to smile up at her as she tucks me in, the blanket to my chin. Fred the parrot goes beneath my arm and her hand combs through my hair over the course another cigarette. The shadows are deep around her face but in the glow of one long drag, I catch a shimmer of a tear. With her last lingering touch she says, *Rest, love,* and departs with a click of the stereo's play button.

She shows up with coffees in the midmorning. She is quiet and just hugs me for a while and smokes. Feeling embarrassed, I sip the black coffee and avoid her eyes, squinting through the screen at the already hot day. But as she watches my profile I can tell that she's worried. With her, "worry" isn't quite the right word, of course. She doesn't think I'll do anything too terribly self-destructive. It's just empathy: pain at seeing me hurt, concern about what is going on inside.

Then she says:

Let's get you out of that apartment.

At the complex, she leaves me in the car while she knocks on the door and, somehow, convinces Samar to go across the parking lot to a neighbor's place.

I'm on my knees on the dirty carpet, swiping CDs, looking around at the cramped apartment, inextricable lives festooned and cluttered. But Serala's a storm of motion, whirling through the place, finding masking tape and rubber bands and by luck or instinct little cardboard boxes, stopping only to touch a match to another smoke and once to put Mississippi John Hurt on the stereo, loud. It's less than twenty minutes before she has things boxed and bagged, labeled and dated, and piled at the door, all the while checking to make sure Samar isn't on her way back.

As we are about to gather the last of my minimal belongings, Serala closes the door on the bleach of California sun and turns me by my arms to face her. She massages my shoulders like a manager does his boxer; she smiles big and though it is forced, it isn't fake.

You ready, champ? She asks, switching one palm to my cheek.

I swallow the tears and nod. *We don't have all day, you know—there's drinking to do!*

And we put on our shades and fill our arms and walk out.

As we pull away, I allow myself a glance at Samar, standing across the parking lot, arms folded, in her pose, glaring—but not with the heat I'd expected.

THROUGH THE LATTER YEARS' PRISM of antidepressants, forays into talk therapy, and a several-year dedication to meditation, I can say that the way Serala engaged the chaotic and dangerous sadness that reared up in me was not orthodox, nor solution-based. She never said to me, *You know, Eli, your behavior is really self-destructive and you should consider talking to someone.* From a psycho-medical point of view, particularly for someone who had already fenced with legions of shrinks and swallowed dozens of trial medications, Serala was decidedly silent on the topic of "treatment," possibly because she had already ceased to believe in a biochemical explanation of her own hurt—and possibly because she did not want a "solution" to her own hurt. She never said so plainly but maybe she didn't even believe in medical explanations for sorrow and rage. And that's not what I needed then, that no-nonsense but delicate talk about "getting help" that anyone might have sat me down for.

I think she saw in me a social and spiritual ailment that she related to far too well and this identification was one of the great comforts of my life, nothing less. She shined this light in my face. There was no reason for how blue I got. I was a healthy, intelligent, well-loved, privileged white man in America and I was merely drowning; it was fucking banal. The more accounts of American-bankrolled genocide in Central America that I read, the more I learned about how deeply my own complicity in the bloodiness of American imperialism ran, the more ruptured my sleep became, the tighter my chest constricted, the quicker I was to useless acts and statements of rage. It was the process of learning that my privilege and comfort comes at a grave cost that others pay. Perhaps the root of my blues has always been biochemical, but if so, the political education I was receiving and the appalling leisure that I, and everyone around me, was living worsened the chemical blue considerably.

Serala made me feel sane and right for hurting, instead of weak, disturbed, melodramatic, and lonely. It was massively comforting to realize that there was someone else in my life that was also laid low by how wrong the world is. Much of my fear bloomed and much of my sadness permutated from watching people waltz through a deteriorating planet and a cutthroat world with shit-eating grins, including many right at my side who were learning about the same horror and injustice. And so I'd felt crazy at times for my incapacity to wear one of those grins consistently, too.

She gave me reason for my pain, sometimes on note cards secreted in my backpack.

We exist amid people doing horrible shit to each other, Eli, and some people can deflect it all. You and I can ignore it, but we can't keep it out of us. It seeps in just like the air out here—and just like the sweet does when we're driving and laughing, too, or listening to Bruce [Springsteen] and drinking something good. It does work both ways, it's just that there's a lot more shit on the whole, love.

I'd stayed with Samar as long as I had—despite the near-violence, the jealousy, the toxicity of our match—because I felt guilty. I was terrified of what would happen if I pulled the trigger: afraid, primarily, that she would hurt herself, either deliberately or unconsciously. And so I chose the path of least resistance and stayed. Suffered, and boiled, and worsened the blackness that was metastasizing in my head and my soul during that time. Again, Serala never had to say it plainly, and if she had, I probably wouldn't have heard it. She said it by action, by ushering me to that apartment to empty it and welcoming me to her space instead: *The hard road is often the right one, and, moreover, the kindest thing you can do for Samar is to leave.* It wasn't a lesson that stuck, sadly, but it was a lesson that freed me from a relationship that might well have been the final ingredient in a volatile emotional cocktail.

Seven

IN THE HOUSE I MOVED into, plastic flapped over broken windows and mysterious roommates had pornographic sex at dawn on the other side of thin walls. Just when you reached the edge of sleep roaches skittered and stuck you full of the willies. In sum, I might have spent ten nights there during the last six weeks of the semester, what with Serala's Batcave always open to me.

It isn't but a night or two after I've "moved" that Serala and Monty and I, all cocked on the cheap booze of a dive bar, stumble back to the Batcave and fall into a heap. Serala is way past done with talk for the night. She slides a Lyle Lovett CD into the stereo and the melody tugs Monty and me quickly toward sleep. I make noises about going home, a slurry promise to stop for a soda to sober up, but she hushes me. *Don't be stupid*, she says, and that's it. I don't know how we all fit, but somehow we three sleep together in her little bed—or Monty and I sleep while Serala watches, most likely. I don't know when the muted but strong animosity I felt toward Monty melted away (because of what his presence in

Serala's life had meant for Jay). Maybe harmony between us was a condition for both of us of retaining her company so we swallowed the pill. But something else was starting to happen, too—I was starting to soften toward Monty because despite his bluster, his politics, he couldn't fully hide that he contained a lot of hurt, too.

Most of those spring nights she left me in her blankets for Monty's room at 3 A.M. or later. She'd kiss my cheek or slide a hand over my head slowly, then turn and walk out with contrary speed. I'd lie there, missing Samar sharply despite the sneers and silence with which she treated me when we crossed paths on campus, but grateful also for the simple words Serala had spoken, or sometimes put onto paper and left waiting for me in the pillows.

You are right, doing the right thing. There is no shame in your struggle, no shame in the pain that you feel. You did not do this to Samar. You did not do anything wrong. She is putting things on you that no one can take off because you are holding onto her through them. But those things are not yours and your love for her will hold its own, you don't have to fill up that place with the guilt she's putting there. That place in you where you love her is still pure and good, and she is taking the dirt from her heart that covered up the sweet y'all had, and putting it on your heart. Don't take it, don't let it cover the purity of what was there, because it still is there, and it won't leave. You don't even have to hold onto that place, it will always be there. And when she puts it there, you have to let go of it, let the wind of this storm blow it out. I promise that wind can't blow the good things out.

The Five Star: a Route 66 dive of red vinyl booths, strong drinks, and smoke you had to wave away to see others. It was a place where a friend would have his car cordoned off in the lot for twenty-four hours while a murder was investigated. It was a blessedly dim place, relatively empty in the early hours. A couple of ruddy-faced barflies always hunched at the bar holding cocktails as if they might try to get away. Sad, mellow blues tunes rasped from the jukebox.

If the outline of the events that haunted Serala was slowly fleshing out, the things that remained mysterious haunted Monty. I recall the way that he looked sometimes in the Five Star when his eyes were glassy, his hands wrapped around a cocktail. I know there was a dead mother and half-told stories of witnessing violence. His father, some kind of international aid baron, had dragged him around to bastions of third world "development" as a child and I don't think that Monty always saw the pretty side. I think, actually, that whatever it was he had seen may have glazed him into the suit of cynicism and drugs that I first knew him in.

One particular night in that glorious dive, Serala is off peeing or getting high or something, and I catch that look on Monty's face, in the way distance has filled up his gaze, and I say something like: *Hey, so I appreciate y'all kind of taking me in. I can always give you more space if you want it, you know.*

And he comes back to the present and blinks, spins his glass and tells me: *No, it's okay, man. She—we—really mean it, really want you around, to take care of you. It's hard times.*

Late that night, in the Batcave, she's off again on some kind of wandering. Monty puts his finger to his lips and digs a black bottle with a rubber stopper out of her closet, opens it—*oops—*

then goes to put it back. But before he can, I snatch it and look into the tarry bottom, smell, for the first time, junk—that balm of hers, that acrid mystery that I will never know. I grimace at the sting of the poison in my nostrils and turn away, not wanting to see where the bottle lives in the Spartan closet.

So Monty pulls out the jar he'd intended to, and takes a snort. His big pale face jerks skyward with a smile that looks like it has been put there by a hammer, and he hands it over. I do the same—and reel several feet to flop on the bed. I see shimmering lines and hear only a glorious ringing, like heaven's trumpets. I laugh hysterically till I come down in what turns out to be about ninety seconds.

Don't tell her, he says with a wink that takes three seconds to effect.

I suppose I didn't. I don't even know what it was.

That is to say that despite his transgressions with her, he was good to me in the ways he knew how and he respected me, I believe. And so there was a particular moment when guilt cranked up high in me . . .

I'm at a kickboxing exam for my third belt. I hold onto this practice despite the fact that it's a three-minute walk from Samar's door. The master is a world-famous fighter and the exercise is hard and good and necessary to keep violence from spilling out of me at foolish moments. I pass the exam and hurry back to campus for some other test in Mexican Politics or Middle East Conflicts or some such thing. But I have to shower and so I stop by the Batcave where I find Serala sunglassed despite the dim room, smoking angrily and stabbing her computer keyboard with an aggression that I can't believe is poetry—but there it is, tumbling to life on the screen. I put an arm around her from behind, intending an abbreviation of a hug, but she grabs it and reaches up for the other.

Did you pass?

Yeah.

I knew you would. She pulls me closer.

I'm super sweaty, I say, because it's true.

I love it, she says, and holds on for a long moment, looking up at me frankly, before I can break away, step into the shower and stare up into the spray of hard water and wonder just what the fuck that was.

THAT WEEKEND, THE HIP-HOP GROUP the Roots comes to perform on campus. It turns out to be a genuine disaster: they show up two hours late, disrespect everyone they meet, demand strong weed (not a problem) and chamomile tea with honey (a bit of a problem) before going onstage. Then they give a mediocre performance until their soundman blows the school's entire speaker system. But I don't care so much because I'm pressed up next to Serala in the surging crowd and I don't have to do a thing but listen and feel her body push and yield with mine.

When the show ends with the explosion of speaker static, we go to meet my father who is visiting. The hallway in the Riverside Inn is dim and thickly carpeted; his room is dimmer. I find acute feelings of both nervousness and excitement about introducing her to him. He lies supine on the double bed, right ankle up on his left knee, stretching the damaged ligaments. There is an old movie on the TV, his pills under the bedside lamp. He doesn't look his worst by any means tonight, but I wish that she could see him when he was younger, thinner, unbroken.

He cuts off the TV and removes his glasses; she sits on the other double bed closest to him and I sit at the foot of his. We are carrying around a bottle of wine and we share it in the tiny hotel cups. I know that we talk about films, about the Roots show and what it says about fame and corruption, and about our dog Sky, a thousand miles north, probably hobbling around looking for Dad at that very moment. I recall all this, though, as more of a feeling than an event; picturing the two of them chatting brings me comfort. I know that for both of them, the other's presence also brings comfort. I know it that night when we leave the hotel and she is quiet for a long time. I know it the next day when he asks more than he ever has about her, as if he were writing a profile.

I DIDN'T FIND IT ODD when Serala became the second person that year, after my father, to suggest we drive to Tijuana. Really let the highway carry us this time, instead of the mere miles between campus and diners. Her objective is the same as my father's was: to get our hands on some painkillers.

The wind and flying cigarette ashes make my study of the British partitioning of Palestine tedious. Somewhere closer to Riverside than Tijuana, I put my texts aside on the empty backseat. Locks of Serala's black hair roll and snap behind her, nearly touching my face. In the shotgun seat is Monty. Björk does her best to escape the static-shot speakers of Desert Storm.

Hustlers take us very quickly to what we want. Monty and I together make short work of the alleys and drugstores with our Spanish skills, honed in points farther south. The white-coated pharmacists sometimes balk; we are more risky clientele than my father, but when we extract larger bills, their scruples crumble and we gather big foil sheets of Vicodin, Soma, and bottles of liquid codeine. In a Corona-pennant and chili-light crowded taqueria, Serala goes to the restroom with the pills; Monty and I buy Gatorade and pour codeine into it.

A few hundred yards shy of the border's razor wire, stern agents, and German shepherds, we split up. Serala checks her watch a lot and is very good at looking exasperated. Monty and I play the role of fatigued tourists. I'm nervous for Serala with all those pills and her dark skin, lip ring, but the agent doesn't even ask her a question when she whips out her ID, like a cop might do with his badge. When the officer asks me if I have anything to declare, I shake my head and take a swallow of the sour red blend. He waves me on.

Later that night, back in the Batcave, Serala doles out Vicodin, lying prone on her elbows with Fred the parrot at her side. Her hands flying over the foil sheets, punching out the tablets, she gives me specific instructions.

If you take three you can drink a little; if you take four you can't. If you take two, I'll tell you when you've had too much to drink.

But even Serala couldn't understand the way that those pills affect me. While Serala and Monty and a redheaded girl all reel into lazy dizziness, I get downright hyper and giddy like I've been snorting coke. Going stir-crazy in the Batcave, I fly out, beer in hand, to the quad, where I run up and down the chemical grass mounds, drop and roll like a child. I find an Asian freshman kid lolling in a hammock and start some kind of deep exchange; I remember hearing the music leaking from Serala's window fifty yards away—Mazzy Star, I think. The night is oddly clear for southern California and the stars are bright. Spring is in effect and it feels good.

We stop at the grocery store for booze and the fluorescent lights are too much so I buy cheap sunglasses, then a big red rubber ball. None of them can figure me out, but I'm not even interested—if I'm having an adverse reaction to painkillers then I'm all for adverse reactions.

At a rowdy party at a beat-up old house, I am in my element with the drunks, flyers-up games with the rubber ball behind the place. It's a while before I realize I've lost track of Serala, and I wander down the driveway. I find her on the front stoop, looking bad, Monty standing awkwardly off to the side, draining a cup of beer. The light from orange streetlamps softly coats her. I ask how she is.

Sick, she says, and when I look at her hunched there, collapsed into half her size and trembling a bit, all my moron high burns off and I realize she's been poorly all night and I have been oblivious. It is literal—she's been puking—but also not so, I think. It is one of the most troubled looks I've seen on her: pallor even on her dark skin, eyes both glazed and wild, like she has witnessed a massacre.

She must have pasted on one of her don't-fuck-with-me faces and strode off to some funky corner of that house to add heroin to the litany swirling through her, because just the pills would have been a mild high. I see her in the bathroom of that old house, the fluorescent light, the odor of rotting pipes and drunk misses of the toilet around her, sloshed assholes pounding the door while she screams *fuck off* and then gets the needle in or the line cut and sucks orgasmic air as the rush turns the room into cloud.

Soon after that night she tried to explain.

Sometimes i feel like i lie even to you. All the things that you don't see. Your pain weighs on me as does Monty's, because it is my own in a way that i failed to ever explain to you. Once i told you, but only half. It's when days and nights pass and I do not move from my bed, i don't open my eyes for more than an hour and still i am not sleeping. And when i do get up it's because everyone and the world has passed through my eyes, then you come back into my sight. And i think, somewhere Eli is doing this. Somewhere Eli is outside in the world and he is fighting and working for himself and things outside himself too. And i live for that, i live through you in ways you probably never imagined. And i say i lie because there is only one part to me, and everything i do and don't do comes from only one place. When i shower i still try to wash off old scars, and when i get out i want to shake my skin off because it's so tight, like a bag that's too full. And it's stupid and wrong because there isn't anything that i don't have. i live for the people i love, out of a certain fairness or unfairness, i live because i am unwilling to put my pain on the people i love. i don't have other parts like you do, but in loving you i have access to other parts, through you.

And in this letter, too, came the confirmation of a suspicion. All that she said: *I once lost someone, someone who was like me, someone I loved more than any child should have to bear. He told me one night, both of us bleeding and crying, that soon he would die.*

And then he did.

That's all she told me.

That's all I know—if I were to speculate, I'd say that he killed himself, this child-lover. I'd guess that he couldn't go on and so he ended it and, as a result, she was imbued with a romantic pull toward that act that would curse her forever.

THREE MONTHS BEFORE OUR SPLIT, Samar and I had adopted the cat, Ché. Quickly after, he is diagnosed with leukemia. His worsening condition keeps pace with the gulf yawning open between her and me. The last time I exercise my visitation rights he's jaundiced, moaning in pain. I finally cajole her to bring him to campus for what I suspect will be my last glimpse. Samar does not look me in the eyes when she dumps him into my arms, just tells me where and when to give him back.

I bring him to the Batcave where Serala is battling her poetry portfolio. She doesn't blink at his condition and she takes a break to sit on her bed with him in the slanting rays of May sun. He is so far gone at this point that he can't move around very well, just stares confusedly at things and makes broken meows. His belly is swollen and his ears are turning yellow. Serala caresses him, gets him settled down into a semblance of comfort for a few minutes. In the Batcave it's like she snatches some moments out of time's hands just for him and I remember hearing him purr.

A FEW DAYS LATER, SAMAR calls. *I'm taking the cat to get put down,* she tells me with the chill and confidence of an iceberg, *so if you want to say goodbye, you better fucking come over.* Ché and his descent toward death is an apt metaphor. I tell her I'd be glad to take Ché to the vet myself, but

I can't make it over. She hangs up on me.

In the end, she stalls too long, and Ché crawls off somewhere for the dignity of a private passing.

SERALA HAD NEVER SHOWED NERVOUSNESS per se, only anxiety from time to time. And she didn't acknowledge it the night of her avant-garde "thesis defense." She just acted pissed off and smoked with a violent hand.

I'm falling all over myself to be supportive and help her but *there's nothing*, she says, shortly. So, dumbly, I go buy her flowers. I catch up to her a few minutes before it starts and she grabs them out of my hands.

Fucking idiot—you're not supposed to buy me flowers.

It hurts even though I understand she is just undone—as well as I understand that buying her flowers was a dumb thing to do. I lean against the chain-link fence outside the presentation hall and look away up to the smog-cloaked mountains. Her face reforms around a conciliatory smile and she takes the time to hug me. Then she drags the bouquet away in a death grip, upside down.

The big room is packed, the floor covered with butcher paper, microphones in different corners, tubes of paint and brushes, projector and screen in the center, huge woofer speakers against the wall. The faculty members are seated at their card table, smiling anticipatorily. Serala rises from her own table and grasps a microphone hard enough that no one can tell she is shaking. I hear it in her voice, though, and happily count it as evidence that I know her best.

Okay, so what I'm going to be doing tonight is basically splicing together all these filmstrips of my work, based upon or in response to whatever you all are doing. Thanks.

Not a lot of preamble. No outgoing-filmmaker/poet-speech; no nostalgia.

Then she sits, the lights go down, the beat drops and a lot of kids on a lot of drugs go at the room. Shirtless hippies smear their torsos with acrylics and roll across the floor; a crew of ravers start their weird dancing. The faculty smiles and scribbles. Jay—who wants her to know that he still cares—kicks the first freestyle raps. And she goes to work—head down, fingers flying, weaving a filmstrip of cached footage to the rhythm of the present madness she has invited.

There is part of me that thinks she conjured this project as a cloaked scoff at Sage Hill, at the fetish of "interpretive, cutting edge" art that people in liberal arts schools tend to wax grandiose about. On the other hand, maybe it was real inspiration, a piece of evidence that despite her derision of the world she inhabited she was very much *of* it—as an artist, at least.

I don't know because I don't remember the final filmstrip. I just sat, watching over her through her discomfort and her art, feeling proud as hell because I had some nascent notion of just how tough it was: to stand under the acid burn of the limelight, believing all her scars and bruises visible, to simply be public, to be gracious— to be wide-open by way of art.

IT WAS ONLY DAYS LATER, the golden hammer of May dropping hard, that she asked me to follow her and Monty across the country. I'd made plans to pick up two old friends from the end of their college careers in Boston and New York. The prospect of looking at the back of Monty's and Serala's heads over a series of days and nights was not one hundred percent appealing. But the ability to decline wasn't in me. She packed up the Batcave in less than an hour, I folded her futon into my new-used Pathfinder (Louis kept the Buick), and we went out for one last Californian night.

I say farewell to Samar at a house party hours later, at the cracked front door. She leans into the rectangle of light and grins and kisses me, mimicking all the goodbyes before—only different. We haven't acknowledged a truce, just somehow moved on. She takes off the hooded sweatshirt I'd coveted and pushes it into my arms.

Take it; it's still cold where you're going.

THE NEXT MORNING, I STRUGGLE to keep sight of Serala's Desert Storm, weaving in and out of the traffic, over the ruts and potholes of I-15, blasting north, under the razor wire—wrapped exit signs, the billboards for bail bonds and plastic surgery, the exhausted sky. I feel some of the freedom that Serala and Monty do, even though I'll be back for my own senior year soon enough. Only minutes down the freeway, she sticks her skinny, scarred arm out the window and starts flashing numbers at me—5, 0, 3, 4. I have no idea what this means. It is hours later in a Nevada truck stop, the sun bleeding away in the land we've left, that I ask.

A radio station, retard, she says, sweetly. *It was just that KXPR was playing "I Can See Clearly Now"—one last time.*

IT'S PECULIAR TO CONSIDER THE willingness with which I made myself a third wheel to Serala and Monty. But then again,

Serala was skilled in a good number of dynamics, not least of all presenting absurd—if interesting—plans as perfectly logical. I was headed to the East Coast to pick up friends? Perfect—I'd just caravan with her and Monty, share some road meals, safety in numbers, maybe a few parties along the way, et cetera. The fact that I was proud to a fault is only a further testament to her ability to frame things compellingly. But all that was only scaffolding; the deeper truth is that I was already deeply under her spell, hungry to gobble up time and space and the world itself in her presence.

I'd shot off for Mexico to smuggle drugs without a second thought; I'd swallowed those drugs with glee. I'd joined Monty in ripping my brain with a mystery substance, and I'd lost weeknights when I should have been studying to loud, sad music and too much wine. I'd done these things not only because I was in a reckless and unbalanced phase in my own life, but to stay in her orbit, to make that orbit tighter, even. It's ironic that I'd do so because Serala was always responsible when it came to others and would have hated to think she was influencing me to damage my liver, fuzz my brain, or bury my blues instead of confront them. She never pushed a drop, or a drag, or a line, or a single capsule on anyone, so far as I know. But the instant that anyone expressed interest in altering their head, she was up for it—searching, supplying, sharing.

Eventually, she enabled years of pleasant fog for me, some of which I regret. If I asked her in the late morning, as I did sometimes as a test, if it was time to start drinking, she always grinned and said, *fuck, yes,* and I'd have to make some lame excuse for why I couldn't really do so. She never bothered with justification. *Life is rough enough without fucking guilt,* she'd say with a cartoonish sneer, cracking the seal on whisky, crumbling hash, throwing back a pill. And I joined her in the measure that I could without derailing entirely because I wanted her to know I was near and that she was not judged, either.

I wasn't overly eager to introduce anyone to my father at that time—he was too broken, too addicted, too sad, and there was a part of me that wanted to protect his image from those who had no point of reference. But the inverse was true of Serala. I wanted her to know my father as quickly and as deeply as possible; I wanted, for both of them, a chance or two to feel less strange and alone, to glimpse the beast of sadness—to say nothing of addiction— turning over inside another soft but durable person. There was bound to be an automatic and genuine kinship there, beyond that which I could share with her because he had lived as an addict and as a manic-depressive for decades. These things alone do not form a kinship of course, but the unconditional love they offered to those around them and the hazardous wide openness to the world it indicated certainly did.

What did not occur to me then was whether their darkness would metastasize within reach of the other's—if by presenting them to each other I was perhaps accelerating my own coming loneliness, the sad charter for my looming adult life.

Part II

Eight

So we drive.

The vulgar flash of Vegas lies ahead. At first, though, it's just a glitter blanket, like a scrap of desert sky cut out and dropped. As we get closer Serala starts to tailgate me, then passes. She's eager, I suppose, to get through Sodom without temptation— God knows what kind of mess she and/or her man might be able to get into there. So we bypass the whole nightmare: the tall billboards proclaiming the cheapest prime rib, the highest stakes, the best cabaret; past the casinos shaped like pyramids, pirate ships, teepees; past the pawnshops with their twenty-four hour neon promise of *next time, next time you'll win*; the marquees large enough to read from an airplane: *Elvis Lives!*

About the time we pull into a trashy motel, I am interrogating my desire—my reason for agreeing to this journey—to be closer to her. What does closer mean? I try to snap my brain closed and enter the room. The blue neon VACANCY sign bleeds through the thin curtains. I watch her and Monty collapse into bed.

I lie on the floor with a beer, scrawling my confusion in a spiral notebook.

MONTY DECIDED WE WOULD BE making a detour: from Denver up to St. Paul to see his brother, a cool thousand-mile tangent. It was then, rolling up the spine of Minnesota, that I really laid into myself:

What the *fuck* was I doing?

But before I got a chance to turn the query on her, she shut me up.

We are at a Thai joint, in the company of Monty, his older brother, and some girl. They are all chattering away. She slides her hand under the table and grabs mine. She flips it over like she's examining it; then she tangles her fingers up with mine and just holds it against her thigh. If Monty leans back, he will see this. But I don't have to hear anything from her anymore. I'll follow her without a discussion of anything at all.

FINALLY WE'RE WHIPPING THROUGH the outer belts of Chicago. We go with Serala's brother, Emet, to dinner in a vegetarian joint on the outskirts of the ghetto. I see us all candlelit and eating bright green falafel, the flames winking through pints of amber beer. Emet is so warm that a part of me wants to stay on with him and be done with the questions of our caravan. He's carefully dressed, a bit of a pretty boy, actually, thirty-odd sweaters gathering dust in a walk-in closet. But he's unpretentious and funny, as at ease discussing *South Park* as Nietzsche. While Monty and Serala have an ill-concealed fight by the restrooms, Emet entertains me with stories of his road trips, as if he's covering for his sister, protecting her virtue by not allowing me to see her strife with Monty.

And then we swallow Dexedrine capsules and begin riding into the northern Midwest, pointed toward Ohio. When we hit the storm at two or three in the morning, we are driving blind. There is too much water to see anything besides the squiggled embers of Serala's taillights and the flashbulbs of lightning all around. I'm thinking we should stop, but I know Serala won't want to.

What my Buddhist stepfather would call my "monkey mind" has been turned loose by the speed and I'm talking a million miles an hour to myself. I want to know it all and I can't fathom the notion that something will happen between Serala and me, nor bear the opposite, so I don't know what I want, and I think that she does, but she won't say anything clearly, and then there's Monty, to say nothing of Jay, and the pitfalls here are many but maybe it's not even an issue because—

BOOM!

The bolt quite literally blinds me. The thunder shakes my truck—so hard that I hear the grinding whine of the transmission, trying to pop out of third gear. Luckily, my fishtail on the asphalt swings me into the empty lane and not the drowning culverts on the shoulder. I'm white knuckled and silent and too frightened to stop. The Zen disciplinarian in the sky has applied a castigating blow to my chattering head. So I stay that way for hours, strangling the steering wheel, rigid, keeping on after Desert Storm, which hasn't slowed a bit.

THE COUNTRY AROUND ELYRIA, OHIO, is quintessential Americana: red barns and rolling fields, intersections with kids selling fruit from plywood stands, signs pointing directions and giving miles to the next town, the roller coaster of blue highway hills. When we get close to Cassie's campus, it's already early morning and full-fledged sun is coming soon. Coming around a corner, though, we hit fog sifting through a grove of trees. A black bird lifts off a gravestone in a cemetery suddenly on the right, cuts across my path. And then there is a car—only it's not a car—right fucking in front of me and I have no choice but to wrench left into the oncoming lane; fortunately it's empty. In my state of mind, twelve hundred miles and twenty hours since the last stop, spun out on speed, gas station coffee, and the psychosis of sleeplessness, the sight is beyond surreal: an Amish family with two children, formally dressed and bonneted, in the carriage with a team of draft horses under the whip of Dad, who wears an Abe Lincoln top hat, his beard like a pelt strapped under his chin. To them, of course, I look every bit as bizarre, with my bare chest, wilding hair, and dilated eyes, my California license plates. I lock gazes with this specter, and when he gives me a strange, three-finger salute, I find myself returning it, as if hypnotized. I knock the gearshift up into third and leave them as far as I can behind, trying to catch Serala's Desert Storm, flying, feeling as if I'm being towed through a dream that teeters on the precipice between nightmare and not.

CASSIE—ALWAYS A CAUSTIC, INSULATED PERSONALITY anyway— is hungover and not terribly glad to see us, it seems. Serala is grouchy and muttering curses at the world; Monty is drowsing; I am trying to choke down Corona so I can fall asleep. I'm glad when I can curl into a corner and will myself to unconsciousness, and I'm glad that when I rise, it's time to go again: on to one of my people in Oberlin. Ohio afternoon light is erasing the eerie memory of the morning and I feel rested despite everything. The setting is all heartland: residential estates; TV antennae devouring the horizon; a barn flattened absolutely, as if fallen from the sky; John Deere machinery parked in duos and triplets, like a meeting of machines; silos, like cocks or missiles, rising all over the passive countryside.

It is a pleasure to see my old friend Gene, but he is distracted by graduation. I recall our time there as a two-day swim through strange parties, lots of beer from those red plastic cups, a house full of black lights, a postmodern art exhibit—but it all runs together. Except for one moment.

It is the morning and we are lounging around Gene's apartment. Gene is out, as usual. We'll be driving again within an hour, and Monty has to hit the store for socks and shaving cream. Serala has put on *The Pretenders' Greatest Hits* very loud. I'm doing my manic calisthenics. I finish and lie down on the floor and she ambles over and lies down next to me. I feel like a child, still and quiet in the dark, hoping the monster he's heard under the bed will just go away. Only my fear is of the way her sudden closeness makes my head swim. Her perfume braids with the cigarette smoke and binds my mind. I'm in a small pouch and she has hold of the drawstrings, closing them. My heart raises its tempo even further when she rolls to me. She's smirking, beautifully, but I don't need to see her eyes to know that there is more than just games in her heart. Monty has been gone all of ninety seconds and she snakes an arm around my neck and pulls herself to me.

I'm sweaty as hell, I say, stupidly.

I told you I love it, she says, and kisses my chest. I disentangle and hop up, hiding my erection with a T-shirt.

I'm going to go take a shower now, I tell her, *because I'm sweaty as hell and because your boyfriend will be back any minute.*

She just smiles and rolls onto her back, lights another Pall Mall, taps a ring on the floorboard to the Pretenders' beat. I get under the cold water cursing her.

She hops in my truck for one hour in Indiana so she can tell me, like a business proposition, over the Beastie Boys' shouts, that *we should have sex if the proper opportunity presents itself.* I cough and scratch my head and study the road through the bug guts on my windshield before nodding.

Good, she says, *now pull over. He doesn't even have a driver's license.* I obey, round the bend of this over-thought ethical question. Just for kicks, I suppose, she sends Monty to ride with me after that.

I BID MONTY FAREWELL WITH a spine-slapping embrace on a Connecticut train platform. An unpleasant mix of affection, nostalgia, disdain, and guilt percolated inside me. I drew myself away so the couple could have a last intimate moment, a handful of kisses, some hurried words, the language of suspended love.

A few hours later, after a diner meal with stilted conversation, too many cigarettes, and the requisite drinks, we walk into her childhood bedroom, and look at each other in the first privacy we've had since California. We sit on the edge of her bed and listen to cicadas sing, rising and falling with a wind from the fallow fields beyond her suburban house. She's fiddling with a lighter, getting up and rifling through drawers, sitting again.

TV, she says suddenly, like an announcement. *TV was the best company when I was a kid. It was always there for me, you know? No better nanny than that.* She speaks loudly and laughs at her own joke, which is unnatural. I know she has decided I will have to start this. I flip off the lamp and put my hand on her neck.

God, what an awkward start. I can see us still: her, the most caustic, forward person I've ever known, the girl that tortured me with innuendo for thousands of miles—her, in that TV-lit bedroom, turning shyly away, whispering: *I'm a big dork when it comes to this part.* Me in the grip of performance anxiety, overwhelmed by the arrival of a moment I've lived in my head many times, finally lying her down and beginning—too tenderly, I think. In the deceptive currents of TV light, the long curves of her bones—her jaw, her clavicle, her cheeks—are like swells in a sea. And I move as I might in a precarious life raft, careful with every inch. We treat each other like we are both virgins and by the time we get the logistics worked out, she arches on top of me, her face now a distant planet, only her thin, double-jointed arms with the scars propping her on my chest. I am half-mast with nerves, scared of her parents waking, distracted by the TV images that silhouette her from behind. She moves stiffly for a while and I'm sure I am boring, terrible, failing at the crucial moment, convinced she is listening to the sitcom. We finish it out with me on top, but it's a Pyrrhic victory by then.

But there is a kind of comfort beneath the blanket that I didn't expect, as if we moved from new lovers to old ones in the space of those few tense moments. She rubs my head and we tangle together, more natural in rest than in lust. The moon rises through the sheer curtains and it cools me, like her hands on me. Lulled,

I sleep the sleep of the dead, like I've had the wildest loving of my life.

When I awakened the next morning, she was gone and the sheets were cool, her pillow squared—in its place. I spent a few minutes squinting at the few photos around the room, trying to learn from these frozen moments of her youth. I willed brightness into my face before stumbling out to greet her mother and the rambunctious chocolate Lab.

But things felt heavy. We had only our separation now, which arrived quickly with my friend Gordon and his NYU duffel bag. Her mother packed us a road cooler, we thanked her profusely, and I hugged Serala quick and hard to skip the threat of tears. But she tugged me aside into the shadow of a pine.

Look, she says, gazing downward at the perfect suburban lawn, *I feel like this isn't the end of anything—not the beginning either.* She scuffs her sandal on the curb, breathes and looks up. *And "this" is nothing that you can define, by the way,* she warns, with the pantomime of a gut punch that makes me flinch. *But I want to know that there's more ahead of us, Eli. I think . . . maybe I even need to.*

I just nod and hug her tight as she wraps those skinny arms around my neck again.

We pull away while the Rolling Stones sing "Under My Thumb" from my tape deck. Next to her beautiful mother, who waves us goodbye, Serala watches from behind her shades, a snapshot of suburban summer.

WE MADE IT TO HER brother's place in time for the first Chicago summer heat wave to roll in like a nuclear blast. We found ourselves lolling around his apartment sweating, smoking bad weed while the most vicious parts of afternoons hung in the sky.

There was this moment there that has stuck with me like an intense or troubling dream: Emet and Gordon are in the living room, talking comic books. I'm in the front room, overlooking the stoop. Emet has just one picture of Serala on his mantle; he keeps things as spare as she does. In it, she is dressed in black and staring the camera down like an adversary. I've just tried to reach her by phone and failed, and so I take the second best option and put my eyes close to her. I'm trying to puzzle her out; I'm trying to figure out if I'm falling in love. The light bulb in the room winks on the photo's gloss, just above her head, like she's having a cartoon idea. She stares back in her defiant way and I can almost hear her say it: *Don't be asinine.* It's what she'd tried to say on her front lawn: *Of course you're falling in love with me, but you ought not insult me or yourself by thinking you know what that means.*

Nine

HUGH AND I HAD TECHNICALLY first met on a soccer field our freshman year of high school. It was one of those late autumn games in the Northwest with pellets of rain like frozen grapes. Everyone was taking a lot of dives into the mud-and-rock mixture that they make soccer fields with, and blood was flowing. I had a temper, and I may or may not have clipped a couple of midfielders a bit hard when I went for the ball. At a break in play, Hugh, who played for the other team, aimed himself toward me. I knew who he and his brother were quite well and I swallowed hard. He was mud-splotched, muscular, square-jawed, and very confident in his power—yet he possessed light eyes that were somehow sensitive. They did not, however, blink when he told me: *Trip another one of my players and me and my brother gonna jump you at school.*

I stepped cautiously into the hallway the next day, but when I crossed paths with Hugh, both of us late for class, I just took a deep breath and stuck out my hand. After he let me sweat for a moment the granite of his face reformed around a toothy and childlike grin. We were sealed thereafter. The anchoring pin of our brotherhood was set later, just days after his brother ended his life, when Hugh called me and a few select others to his family's home. I sat on his brother's bed and mixed my cigarette ashes with his last ones. I leafed through the artwork and journals that he'd left behind, bound with string in a folder, "The Pages of Truth and Love." I held onto Hugh when he finally broke and his thick body shook in my arms.

After that, there had been nothing to prove to each other (though we would prove loyalty, quite literally, with blood, sweat, and tears). There was only the question of growing to expect the other's presence, at the best moments and the hardest. Hugh was there every day that I asked him to be while my father languished in that god-awful hospital; Hugh was there to sit silently with a heavy hand on my shoulder, there to stare down nurses who treated my father badly, there to kick through the front doors at the end of visiting hours and go drink and rage in the nostalgic nests of our city parks.

But there was little in our history richer or better than the afternoons in June and July of '99, full of color, running on young legs.

We figured it out real quick: the land that my mother owned in the Cascade Mountains was abandoned and in need of a lot of attention. My mother and stepfather were making comments about moving there. Hugh, though forged by the inner city, seemed to be a grizzled mountain man by nature. Once he spent a few weeks up there and his body turned brown with sun and dust, his eyes got even lighter, and beard rioted across his face and neck, it was hard to imagine him anywhere else. He had a lot of healing to do still, because glimpsing his brother's ghost at every turn in the city, watching his parents' marriage crumble under so much grief, had prevented much of it.

So, suddenly, Hugh and I had unsupervised jobs to do in a place that was as close to home as I had. We were free, taking long hikes up ridges and hurtling back down, We were wild as the early summer flowers—the mule's ears, the lady's slipper, the Indian paintbrush, the bluebells—that we trampled in our descents to the cold, emerald pools of the Wenatchee River, thousands of feet below.

I LIKE TO THINK SERALA cooked up the idea of moving to Seattle while sleepless and missing me. But it was just as likely born of caffeinated conversations between her and Cassie in a diner, or racing down the back roads of Connecticut in June.

Monty, she claimed, was no longer a factor, just like that.

The night that they are due to arrive Hugh and I quit early at our efforts at turning a nineteenth century homestead into firewood and head down to the swimming hole to bathe.

But they are coming—their caravan of Desert Storm and a big U-Haul—through wicked western storms. Night arrives long before them. By the time they appear in the small hours, both Serala and Cassie are frayed, and Cassie is more than ready for sleep. Hugh passes out, too, but Serala and I are awake, kissing in the gray mountain pre-dawn.

We're tangled in flannel sheets in a tiny room. Her eyes are ravenous while her hands roam over my body, but it's not a sexual need, really. It's more like we need to touch one another to make sure the moment isn't dream. She's on top of me like the first time back in Connecticut, but now we're clothed and I can see her clearly in the swelling morning: locks of hair have slipped the wooden clip and flop down over one eye; she shakes them aside and leans forward, her forearms on either side of my head, till our faces are inches apart. Her stare is absolutely transparent, vulnerable, and insecure—she is undone, I suddenly understand, by where she finds herself.

Are you glad for this? She asks, so close that I can't get away with anything but the truth. I nod, keeping that truth vague and the small doubt muted. *Good,* she breathes and lets a cautious smile unfold. I put my hands on the small of her back and she shuts her eyes in what looks like rest. Her lips are on me as the first ray of dawn cuts through the glass into my eyes and I finally close them.

BACK IN THE CITY, MY father had just remodeled his basement into an apartment, forming a triplex out of his house. When he heard Serala was moving out, he postponed renting so she and Cassie would have a temporary base while they searched for something permanent. Meanwhile, the couple that had lived upstairs in the mother-in-law apartment suddenly moved away. Despite all common sense, the upstairs was handed over to eighteen-year-old Luke for a while.

My brother Luke and I had been on rough terrain: he was doing a lot of drugs; I was being a judgmental and falsely authoritative big brother. He basically wanted me to fuck off and I basically wanted him to listen to me.

We'd been able to set all this conveniently aside for the last couple of years, as he stepped into teenagehood and we had the crisis of dad's accident to unite us. But it was coming time for us to settle up for ugly epochs behind. He was finally done taking shit from me and was, rather, waiting for me to apologize—or at least begin to treat him with respect. But in this era, I wasn't in touch with my crimes. All I knew for sure was that our father was on a precipitous descent into addiction and Luke was, once again, about to shrug free of it all and shove off for half a year of traveling abroad while I was to juggle college and Dad. In my heart, I wanted to make up and go with him, of course, but there was no proclamation of heart's truths between Luke and I then.

It was the Fourth of July, 1999, when my dad and I drove north to get me a golden retriever puppy. He was weaving the Subaru from his OxyContin high.

That night there is a party at high school friends' house. I show up early to catch up with my people before the place is all elbows. I find that my former best friend, Dean, is there, moving around the edges of the scene in a trench coat and sunglasses. Dean and I had split when our mutual love for LSD, adrenaline, and spiritual exploration tripped hidden wires in him and his latent schizophrenia bloomed like a fungus. I'd held on as long as I could but just about the time I'd headed off to college, his paranoia had turned him against me and we'd left things sour. So this night, Independence Day years later, we greet one another warmly—explosively in fact, so warmly that one might suspect the veracity of the warmth. In the early evening, Seattle going all blue like it does in the summer dusks, I walk outside and see Dean with my new puppy, Kaya, in his arms, a huge grin on his face, her sleeping soundly as he rocks her like a child. It unnerves me, deeply.

Serala appears later with Cassie, both of them aggressively uncomfortable, overcompensating with swigs from a half-gallon of Jack Daniel's. I soon lose her in the swirl of people. When things get too hectic in the backyard—blotto boys are lighting high-powered firecrackers that tip over and blast into the crowd, sending bodies diving—I come inside to find her again.

She's in an upstairs bedroom with a handful of others; it's opaque with weed smoke and I'm unhappy, firstly, to find Kaya sneezing in the corner. When I glance over and see that Serala is holding hands with Dean, the scope of the rage I feel is immense, irrational, and instant. Dean chuckles at me with his eyes. I imagine that I recover enough to shake my head at Serala. She says something like: *Hey, maybe you shouldn't be so judgmental. There's a lot he has to say to you, to offer.*

Dean smiles at me with uncontainable glee, mock-innocence widening his mouth and eyes. Maintaining composure requires me to stay for a hit of the pipe, but I leave quickly and I leave her with a blade of a glance.

I was in that boozy twilight zone where an emotion flows pure and fast. I was on my way—foolishly—to my car when she caught me. The street was deserted and the party sounded like a distant reality. A yellow fingernail moon hung with a trio of stars. A breeze ushered me up the block but she caught up, a terrible desperation in her face, as if she thought I was leaving her forever. I knew then that Dean had somehow connived her into saying what she did; she was horrified at the prospect of having betrayed me. But I still wanted to punish her.

What is it, what? I'm sorry, what is it?

I look at the sickle of moon and frown, shake my head.

You have no possible fucking way of knowing how bad that was.

She has her hand tight on my arm, nearing tears now. Countless phrases that I could hurl tumble in my mind, ways I could make her grovel and fight. I have power over her—this sudden epiphany drops the floor out of my mind because I've never really seen anyone exercise control over Serala. Do I trust myself enough for this? To not hurt her when I can? When, in some vague way she seems to be asking for it?

I'm sorry, I'm sorry. Forgive me.

I do.

A WEEK LATER, LUKE'S HIGH school graduation ceremony is mercifully short and unorthodox; unlike me, he's attended an alternative high school, a "progressive" place where they prize creativity and social works. Afterward, a tall bombshell sidles up to me.

I guess you're Luke's brother, huh?

I swallow my surprise at her approach.

I'm Heidi's sister, Abigail.

I wouldn't have guessed this; my brother's ex-girlfriend Heidi is pretty, but not quite in the ballpark of this creature. She wants to know what's going on tonight.

The night goes well over whisky and innuendo and I convince her that her boyfriend back in California is a jackass—recklessly, not caring, tunnel vision—and she agrees to come home with me. We make a glorious mess of the apartment, Luke fortunately out on another nightlong ecstasy ramble. We have coffee in the morning and I take her home; she's as nonchalant as Serala seems to be. But the moment comes to test that the next day as Serala and I are stuck in U-District traffic, her smoking and banging on the horn, earning looks of disapproval because that's something that drivers simply do not do in Seattle.

So I took this hot girl home the other night.

Serala turns to me, DKNY glasses blocking any guess at her reaction. After a minute she turns back to the road, traffic moves, and she takes a drag.

Good for you, fucker.

Are you mad? I mean . . .

I leave off here, at the trailhead to everything I would have to say if I misread her policy.

No, but don't expect me not to be a little bit jealous, she says, wheeling fast around the corner, unable to keep the smile off her face now. And then, once more before we are at her and Cassie's new apartment where we go to make love, *Good for you.*

In August, Jay returned from Teach for America in Texas. The back of my mind had been a hectic place these last weeks. I didn't know what to expect; all I knew was that I hadn't received a response to the letter I sent, telling him that Serala and I were, well, closer.

At his parents' condo he greets me and Kaya with all the gregarious love he always has. We take to the porch and talk about Texas, and teaching, and all of our scattered friends. The summer sun does its work on our heads till we are lulled toward sleepy and go back inside, leaving Kaya wrestling a piece of rawhide on the deck.

I'm feeling determined to not bring it up. Finally he does so with a sigh.

Yo, so in terms of all that with you and her, man, really—he pauses here to shake his head at me—*I just don't really give a fuck.*

I should be glad at this, of course; of course, I'm not. *Fuck*—the casual violence of that word, still not worn away. But it seems to me it's intentional here anyway, that he wants me to read it as code—but for what? Yes, I'm pissed but I'll handle it? Yes, I'm pissed and you should knock it off even though I'm not telling you to? I'm hurt but I've hurt you before, so I'll get through it? Or is it possible that he really doesn't care because of the emotional distance he's shoved between Serala and himself?

I mean, truly Eli, the only thing I'll say is that I just worry about you.

When Jay falls silent in a certain manner, one knows that one is supposed to urge him on. On some level I know what I am seeing: the inverse of and yet the same thing as what I saw in his dorm room over two years earlier. All of the hurt—so strong it became fear—that had consumed Jay when Serala left him had scarred over into bitterness, disdain. Jay never has said or done things halfway; his passion burns at the center of his words, his life, his music, and his relationships. If he doesn't get to be in love with her, then the disdain will have to be just as white-hot. It isn't hatred, of course, because he will always love Serala.

He looks at me with reined intensity in his wide eyes, broad brow furrowed, waiting for the nudge. KRS-One hollers between bass lines from his bedroom.

Okay, Jay, but what do you mean?

And he takes in a breath, sits up, and shrugs his shoulders. This is it: the response he selected to that crummy letter I sent weeks ago.

She's just hard, man. She's a very negative person and all that shit is really seductive, but it's also toxic. I know because I felt it and fell to it, you know, for a long time. It's taken me a long time to get distance from it. But it's hard to not get wrapped up in it, even as a friend. On the level of sex, or romance, or what-the-fuck-ever, it's even more so. Just be careful, you know?

I'm not you, Jay.

It comes out encased in more ice than I would have chosen. But he just shakes his head again, resigned, like a recovered alcoholic talking to an up-and-coming one. And so I nod, because I'm not about to get into a philosophical debate about Serala—and because I'm not entirely sure that he is wrong.

Kaya, done with the rawhide, smacks the glass door with her paw and yips once, just a pantomime through the thick pane.

THAT SUMMER IS JUST MAINLY composed of fucking and eating and laughing: trying to keep our sex quiet because Cassie's in the living room and failing so we laugh instead; watching Kaya stalk Cassie's cat around the apartment; wine and hanky-panky before the woodstove of the mountain house, the Cascades' breeze as evening falls; sitting at cafés, eating and drinking; watching old movies with my father; walking my old dog Sky slowly down the block; holding each other late into the morning while Etta James albums play, whorls of dust motes in the sunrays.

I remember the good things more acutely than the bad. But I remember, also, the awful moments, when sleep was too distant for too long, when I was absent for days and, I'm sure, she bit the hook of heroin again. I remember the wild beauty of her eyes inverted into wild terror when she awoke from nightmares, the long seconds it took to bring her back. But we were glad even for this, because it meant she had plunged all the way into the sea of sleep, not merely dipped a toe and recoiled into red-eyed empty hours, as was typical—her sleeplessness was a given and she never seemed intent on talking about it much. I wrote her letters and delivered them by hand, hoping they would mean more on paper.

> *. . . You know . . . how much I want to lift your pain away. I obsess about it sometimes; it's always itching in my mind somewhere. And nothing can make me smile broader than hearing you laugh genuinely or tell me without that "listen, I just gotta bullshit you" look in your eye, that you are doing well. I've managed to accept that most of the time I won't get to smile at how happy you are, and I can live with that. I'm real clear that I can't part any proverbial clouds for you and I guess that's good. It doesn't keep me from dreaming about finding you The Cure. It all even goes beyond you; it permeates my discussions with God. I ask how can it be that you have to suffer so much. I ask for justice for my friend with the heart of gold and tormented soul. I lose track of the faith that I harbor about my own pain and struggle. It seems like too much and sometimes I even slip into rages about it when I know that you are on a descent. I cannot pretend to know the scope of your pain and I cannot pretend to have any airtight philosophical explanation for its merciless poisoning of you . . .*

My empathy opened her wider to me, it seemed, imbued her with the need to explain more, better, differently. And she welcomed my love when it came in these expected containers, but she was clear that it did not alter her world.

> *Some days i can feel the distance, and everything, every cell inside and out of me proves that i'm moving further away. That i'm too different, because even dissidents and viruses have their place in the big cycle of everything. And it spins faster, and gravity pushes me out toward the edges and stuck against walls. Like at any moment, it will cut me loose and all the force of gravity and math and physics will come together in perfect sync, in nature's cycle and throw me out. 'Cause i'm not part of it, not even the small cycles inside me work . . . but i wish i could just speak or write and tell you, 'cause i think there are things you know more than me, and i always believe you somewhere inside (even when i have a quick negative to spit out).*

In the last days of that August, I was in the mountains with Hugh, and my childhood friend Billy, at work for my stepfather on the homestead-turned-woodpile. On a Thursday, we quit early, swam in the river and split for a concert at the Gorge, a breathtaking amphitheater on the banks of the Columbia River. An absurd and unfortunate series of events—beginning with Billy accidentally blowing a bowl of charred weed onto the chest of a rent-a-cop—landed me in the slammer for the entire three-day weekend on a felony charge for possession of psilocybin mushrooms.

My first morning incarcerated, after forcing down the dribbling yellow mess they called eggs, I dial Serala's number. But it's sweet, morning-baffled Cassie that answers and accepts the "charges coming from a correctional institution," instantly on task, asking what she needs to do. I tell her not to worry and put Serala on the phone. But Serala isn't in.

As I sit against the wall in my orange jumpsuit and watch the prisoners give meaning to the day in their various ways, I can tell who the junkies are—versus the tweekers, the crackheads, the drunks, or simple thugs. They slump in cells, quivering a little but bored, not playing cards, or holding forth, or slap boxing like the others. Mainly, it seems, they are just waiting.

I'd been gone for several days from Seattle and I wondered how many Serala had been gone from her bed.

It was a heady and baffling time that appears now more exhausting than alluring, but then felt like pure, uncut life flowing into my mainline vein. I sure as hell didn't know what it meant to fall in love with Serala, but it was like electrified carbonation instead of blood in me. All my life, like most people, I'd observed the opposite sex in customary straightjackets: strictly friend, strictly fling, or unhealthy, fraught, long-term relationship. It was thrilling to discover another category and that the category was real—lots of people talked about "fuck buddies" and "friends with benefits" but few of those supposedly easy affairs landed right side up. And, besides, that didn't even begin to articulate what was taking place. I was learning what nonpossession meant, enjoying the inverse of the high-octane poison of jealousy that had produced so much drama and pain in my life. I had endured a vicious blow of jealousy when I found Serala stoned and intimate with Dean at the house party, but the betrayal was intellectual, spiritual even—she'd offered her ear to a person who'd once turned against me despite my loyalty to him. If I'd walked in on her tangled naked with a random boy, I probably would have excused myself and split for a few hours.

I'd told Jay (too sharply) that *I wasn't him* when he'd issued his echoing warning—*careful man, she's very negative, it's toxic*—because I knew I wouldn't fall into the trap of conventional love with Serala as he had. For me, to love Serala was to oppose her cynicism and to hope for change, goodness, justice, salvation. I had no perspective to see what that definition of love implied: that I was suddenly and deeply engaged in a fight that would be very difficult to continue from afar—the ceaseless fight, waged with words and music, food and sex, to convince her that she was wrong and this life is worth it, in the end.

I did not have the vision to consider that when one wades into pitched battle with concepts such as "hope" as battle standards, one is necessarily conceding that they can be bloodied—and lost. That's what Jay, perhaps, was trying to tell me.

Ten

In September I followed Interstate 5 away from Serala and Seattle, back to school with a groan but some excitement too. Kaya roamed around the truck curiously, I played Serala's mix tapes and tried to convince myself I could write my thesis in one semester.

When I pull into the gravel driveway of my new home, trust fund hippies and loud girls are splayed all over the front porch. I haul my bags in through a crowd of pool players, only half of whom I know, into the tiny bedroom that has been saved for me, to find it brimming with my new roommate's overflow of belongings.

Don't sweat it, bro, I'll move it later, he says, swaying in the doorway, *I've got a steak on the grill for you.*

That charms me. Kaya charms everybody, and thus the year begins.

I met Mona, a pretty Persian girl in a hippie blouse and pigtails in downtown Riverside. I was outside a bar with Jay, drinking beer in the crisp autumn air. Mona floated down the avenue with her shy dog. The gusts of afternoon took hold of her black hair and showed me her huge Eastern eyes, which suddenly became the only things on the block. Jay called her over. She split her attention between me, him, and her dog, which she stroked constantly, like it was as natural as breathing. I kicked Jay under the patio table and was introduced, told we were actually neighbors. She smiled and told me that she guessed she'd be the girl next door.

She happened by my big, dirty party house frequently with her dog, which Kaya fell in love with. I liked the situation, but I also liked her a lot more than I was willing to admit; she was beautiful, apparently mellow-mooded, easy to talk to, right next door. She was a highly sensitive, tentative cynic with a warm heart. The fact that she was the third Middle Eastern woman to capture my attention in the last few years was curious. It was somewhat problematic as it was bound to get me shit dealt by observant friends, but not nearly enough to put a stop to the carnal momentum.

I STARTED ON THE MONSTER thesis on the national politics of Venezuela.

The police killed an unarmed black man under suspicious circumstances and a protest movement erupted among both the Pan-African Student Association and their white peers, like me, swollen with liberal guilt.

The fight began to unionize the dining hall workers.

Every time I called, my father answered the phone with increasing loopiness, tumbling further into depression, pain, and drugs.

My only response to all this was my angst-ridden poetry, which I was taking as seriously as a heart attack.

And then there was Serala's descent.

I spent hours on the filthy sofa on my porch, the cordless pressed to my head, listening with increasing alarm. I pushed her toward my father. I imagined them sharing some wine, staring out at the streetlights on the bridge, Neil Young in the background. Or watching some good flicks and making each other feel more real, more human, more hopeful. I preferred not to think that, instead, they sat around and got lifted together, sharing pills or even junk, feeling safe and easy and less ashamed for the company and maybe, also, pulling each other haphazardly toward a peace I wasn't ready to condone as their destination, like two drunks helping one another foolishly and inevitably toward their car under a moonless sky.

Serala filled her days with extra shifts at a record store, and with long, circuitous drives around all the bodies of water, playing her way through Lyle Lovett, Lucinda Williams, Nick Drake, Gillian Welch, Portishead—all the sounds that recognized the pain inside of her. But it was like trying to stop the pulsing spurt of an artery with a napkin: the autumn was cutting her down and I heard it.

Then I got a letter, which I've lost along with too many others.

First, she is followed by a drunken frat boy who hollers obscene demands as she is walking home. She lights a Pall Mall to show she's not scared, gives him the finger over her shoulder, moves under the streetlights. But he's too far gone to care, stalking her boldly, hollering crude questions. When she is near her door, he takes some quick steps and throws her against a wall.

Now you're gonna fuckin' pay attention to me, he slurs, hands like cold fish flopping around her blouse. So she maces him and pushes him off, him screaming in agony, she says, and I believe her. I can see her white teeth clamped with rage like a jaw floating in the absolute dark, her left hand biting crescents into his chest as she holds him steady to hit him directly with the chemical spray. I can see that, but her pretense of laughing it off rings hollow.

And not two days later, the same street, trudging home from another shift, she finds a dog, crushed by a driver who has fled. The dog is crying quietly through his last moments. I can see her sit down on the curb, put her smoke out, and hold that dog, rocking, as he takes his last, heaving breaths. I can see tipsy diners, wandering back to their cars, standing over her, asking with their meager curiosity *what's happened, what's wrong,* and being treated to a hiss of warning to *fuck off.* I wonder what spirit might have been in that dog, so unlucky to die that way, so fortunate to die in her arms—like others, before then and still to come.

When we'd made plans to meet in Frisco during a school break in October, we were both relieved to have in our minds a day, an hour, a place stamped: a promise of relief up the highway.

Serala looks good when she comes through the doors of baggage claim, wearing a headscarf and jeans—more casual than usual— and her eyes are bright, not even shielded behind sunglasses. I have Kaya with me, who goes bananas, squealing and racing in circles around her legs, peeing everywhere to the chagrin of the skycaps.

We go to bed early in a trashy motel and when we make love it is different; it feels like we have been saving it up and, simultaneously, like we are trying to make it suffice for all the coming distance. And when the blanket slides away, when we wake the puppy and she cries softly, it is, perhaps, because the event is like a separate physical being in the room with us.

Those few days it was as if she'd been exonerated of some capital crime and was entering the world again, free. This was escape, vacation, and comfort; this was her respite from what was taking her apart, piece by piece. It is all images and emotions that I recall, until the very last moments, which I have still, as tenacious as a splinter, lodged in my mind:

On the sun-washed skull of parking structure C she wears black—more formal again, returning. To the north Frisco broods invisible under its shroud. Strands of freeway whine and thunder in the west. Jumbo jets lumber into the cobalt sky, so close that Serala's hair lifts. The wind blows from another direction, so her hair lifts that way too, frenzied. Gusts break the ashes from her cigarettes and hurl their nothingness against the loud canvas of the world. But she is very calm, or at least her hands don't shake when she drags on the cigarettes. Kaya runs in gleeful circles, sniffing oil spots and watching birds, giddy to be out of the cheap motel that held us till afternoon. Behind us is the trio of easy days that we carved out of places like Half Moon Bay and Santa Clara. Nothing was half or saintly or clear about any of it. I remember awaking to folds of ocean on rocks, the hiss and explosion of breakers, thinking she had just said something important. But there were only her eyes and perfect teeth, the sliver of a kiss, and she sent me back to dream. It was all lovemaking, and eating, and driving that made it feel like escape instead of a weekend.

Suddenly all that is left is a walk to the elevator. God, the frayed conviction in those eyes! The stride of those black boots! As the doors close I blow a kiss and she looks down. And I am alone on that rooftop with my dog, and my truck, and the wrath of a merciless October.

Two days later, carrying the poetry book I'd bought as a gift, I knock on the door to Mona's bungalow and we both say *hi* at once, nervous. She invites me in and her dog, Kasko, checks me out like a bouncer. When small talk falters, she grabs me with a confidence I wouldn't have guessed at. We go at each other, blowing away my notions of her as demure, sweet, somewhat passive. The dog sits at attention and gives me a chilly glare as we gasp back to life. When Mona sees me looking out the window she says: *It's okay, you know, you don't have to stay.* So I get up and split straight off, scared of the mild commitment of a few hours in her bed.

When I scale the wobbly fence between my house and Mona's, I find the lights are still up and bass lines thunder and billiard balls click. Jay is there, in town to perform with his hip-hop group that's still holding together. He ascertains where I've just been with a glance.

Booty call! He announces and giggles in an infectious way so that all his comrades do, too. With an arm around my shoulder— *C'mon, bro, I'm almost never here, you know, I miss you!*—I agree to stay up with him for a drink. We settle onto the rotting sofa and I feel myself bracing. Prodded by Guinness and the fact that he knows I've spent the last weekend up north with Serala, he tries to draw me into a philosophical argument again.

Do you think the way she looks at shit is right, man? Do you?

Jay's skinny arms wave the question around me like smoke. The tattoo of a fat-faced sun that he got when we were sixteen peeks at me from beneath a sleeve.

I'm not going to have this debate with you, Jay, I say and turn away to underline it.

Why not? What is it that you're afraid of? He drains his pint and levels his eyes at me, willing me to give just a foothold. *She's all negativity, man, and I don't want to see it in you—I don't want to see you go all dark the way I did. You're a light, Eli, and you've got to stay that way.*

Soon he gives up, leaving me with a resigned embrace.

THAT NEXT MONTH, SHE STARTED slipping precipitously and I fought her at every defeated phrase; I promised that it would all be better by Christmas; I returned every volley of despair with a salvo of pep, with faith, however contrived. And sometimes with guilt: *you can't do this to me, you can't do this to your momma, you've got to hang on.* I hung up and hammered the walls with fists, hurled billiard balls into the sofa, drank stabs of whatever rotgut my roommate had around. I talked angrily to her picture, which didn't talk back.

But one November night she told me over the scratchy phone line, in language slowed and dumbed by heroin, that she had a huge spool of string rolling around in the trunk of Desert Storm.

When that spool unwinds completely, she said, *when that spool runs out.*

I knew what that meant and so I bought a plane ticket.

When I got to her apartment, Serala couldn't even raise a smile to welcome me, just spun and walked away from the open door, back to the sofa from which she peered out bitterly. Soon she had traded silence for vitriol.

What the fuck does everyone want? Nobody can read a newspaper and then tell me to cheer up; nobody's going to make me feel crazy. If it's not crazy out there, whirling around and fucking covering everything, infecting everything, why the fuck is it crazy inside me? Everyone else is fucking crazy.

She flopped onto her back and blew out a plume of smoke with a couple drops of saliva. I was pacing, unnerved, and stopped over her.

I don't know, Serala, I said, trying to be genuine, *but I came here to help you figure out how to be crazy enough to get by, I guess.*

No, you fucking came here for yourself, you came here to make yourself feel better—I know that.

She scoffed deep in her throat and turned to face the sofa, as red flapped in the corners of my mind: how dare she? Did she think it was fucking easy to love her? I stormed out of her apartment, barefoot, stopping on a cold corner and breathing steam up into the vapor lights of the International House of Pancakes, almost fighting a drunk who chuckled at the spectacle of me.

I drove Serala the next morning to a hospital because a Connecticut shrink needed her blood for tests. We walked out of there an hour later, her with the cotton ball taped over her mainline. Idly, I picked up a leaf, blood red but tinged with live green around the edges and gave it to her. She cast it aside.

It's just going to fucking die, what do I want with it?

We drove to the house in the mountains. I was happy to buy strong weed and plenty of wine. We cooked the grass into a lackluster cake and she chugged wine and took her sleeping pills, the heavy kind that would have put me out for days. She kneeled by the woodstove, her curtain of blue-black hair swung down over her face, one hand in a fist, banging a thigh, the other throttling a bottle of cabernet. She wept and talked nonsensically until her eyes got heavy and I looked into the fire and prayed that she would sleep. Eventually she did. I carried her into the bedroom and buried her beneath many blankets. I sat by the fire, pretending to study politics. I watched swirls of flame devour the last dry wood of the summer.

When she woke she was quiet, and her hands didn't shake, and I could breathe a little. And she might have even laughed once before we pulled into the city.

We were parked outside her apartment building and the winds whirled leaves and trash down the sidewalk. Pinheads of rain pocked the windshield and we were quiet, failing to be casual in our intent to not be fatalistic. I remember that Serala took the leaf I'd given her the day before from the floor of the car. She seemed surprised to see it hadn't browned and died. She offered me a nod as if to say: *It's enough, for now. Just enough. I will stay with you.*

BUT IMMEDIATELY UPON MY RETURN to Sage Hill there were big plans stewing. The World Trade Organization, the international regulatory body tacitly responsible for enforcing the growing gulf between the rich and the poor of the world, planned to hold a ministerial in Seattle at the end of the month. Almost every professor proclaimed support for participation in a momentous confrontation, a chance to leave the classroom and hit the streets.

I scrambled for another ticket and headed north again to march with what would turn out to be seventy thousand people. My father picked me up at the airport and drove me to the periphery of the madness, dropping me off with a shake of his head. He wasn't thrilled that I was putting myself in the midst of what might turn into a frenzied stomping, and he didn't think it advisable to get arrested while I was awaiting trial for felony possession. He stopped me with a hand on my elbow before I jumped out of his Subaru. The intermittent anemia had chalked half his face and his dark eyes were a little glazed with narcotic, but they were steady. Wind coming up from the Sound, through the crowds, lifted what was left of his hair off his scalp and he smiled at me, giving up on a warning or a lecture.

Good luck down there, he said. And I knew that if it weren't for his broken body, I would be able to cajole him down there at my side and that parts of him he'd long forgotten would have come alive.

A ribbon of humanity as wide as Denny Way, as long as a mile, was visible over the guardrail.

NOVEMBER 30, DAY TWO OF what would come to be called "The Battle in Seattle": I find myself on the piers of the waterfront, which is roiling. A steelworker rally draws a crowd of two thousand or more: steelworkers, college kids, street-living punks, indigenous rights activists, environmentalists, day laborers. The mass begins to march. The emotive impact of crossing the threshold into the heart of Seattle is great; shouts rise higher, faces appear miniscule in the top floor windows of skyscrapers. Construction workers lean off scaffolding with thumbs-up signs. Everything is motion and sound. There is a contingent of drummers banging out rhythms. Smiles grace even bruised faces; rage is obscured. Dance and song rule. Everyone knows that this is what the week is supposed to be about. At last we have gotten it right. And there isn't a cop in sight.

I will always be able to see that armored personnel carrier fishtailing around the corner. Like a massive, robotic insect, something from a late night sci-fi flick, it skitters, then regains its purchase and barrels forward. Commando-dressed cops cling by one arm to the speeding machine. And then it stops. Foolishly, along with dozens of others, I stop too, midway across the avenue. The faceless police level their arsenal and fire into our midst. Objects hurtle across a gulf of ten feet: "bean bag" projectiles, rubber coated bullets, CS gas canisters, and concussion grenades. A rubber bullet grazes my collarbone; a young kid alongside me isn't so lucky—a concussion grenade nicks his temple before it explodes. He spins, bleeding, onto the concrete.

Our ranks have split and fractured, the alleys and side streets alive with frantic scrambling and shouts. But, swiftly, the bulk of us reassemble along the hazy spine of Second Avenue.

As the initial clouds of gas begin to lift, the poison spins around rooftops and flocks of pigeons limp into the air. Anger replaces the terror and pain. Not a face is showing anymore; bandanas, ripped clothing, or gas masks obscure them. The screams begin to coalesce into something whole; voices gather again and rise into one chant from countless sets of scalded lungs: *Whose streets?! OUR streets! Whose streets?! OUR streets!* And we march southward, fists in the air against the rain and gas. And for some moments it is true; it is literal. They are our streets; the police have vanished.

But soon they attack again. It is an onslaught, replete with up-close and personal violence—nightsticks connect volleys of weaponry like hyphens. The end is en masse incarceration, and eventual booking and nasty abuses at King County Jail. Giddy with sleep deprivation and the tear gas fumes, I call Serala from yet another jail, wearing yet another jumpsuit. Yet again, she is not in.

By the time I am released, the protests have triumphed: the corporate bigwigs tucked their tails between their legs and left Seattle, vowing never to return. I call Serala as soon as I have my hands on my cell phone.

She appears on the edge of the scene outside county lockup, a contrast to the wet, filthy, red-faced protesters. She is wearing black again and she is sunglassed, despite the winter gloom. She hugs me tightly and we go, fittingly, to a high-end bar where she buys me a cosmopolitan and we sit, hunched together against the eyes of the bartender and the stray activists and businessmen mixing in the streets.

You know, I'm real proud of you, she says, compensating for the sentimentalism by staring up at a golf open on TV. *You did good.*

It wasn't about me, I retort. *It was about thousands of people standing together.*

I expect a roll of her eyes, a cynical swipe, but she just nods and looks at me briefly, blows smoke past my face and leans over to hold me. She's so thin that her bones feel like knives wrapped in cloth.

I wouldn't have been strong enough for this if it weren't for you, I say, which is true, but also an appeal. But she pulls away and shakes her head vigorously. She wants no part in the celebration. She just kills her cosmopolitan and kisses me. She wants nothing, it seems, and I feel resentful because I want to relish this. And she thinks I can enjoy it without her. And I suppose I do.

ONLY TWO AND A HALF weeks later, winter vacation, I fill my truck with a pair of Seattle boys, Kaya, luggage, and head north for the third time in two months. My goal is to do the drive in one stretch.

At three in the morning, a stone's throw from Oregon, I am in my zone, smoking and feeding beef jerky to Kaya, playing Serala's mix tapes while my two passengers sleep. The freeway has been empty for miles, so when a pair of headlights races up on me I am certain I've blown by a trooper—going eighty—and now it is going to get interesting. I am two weeks from trial for the mushrooms and not entirely sure what my passengers might be holding. Then the approaching car splits apart in my rearview, momentarily jarring my tired mind; I think I'm hallucinating. But it's two sport bikes, one passing me on the right, the other on my bumper, so I swing right when the first one is clear, and the second rides up parallel with me. He is on a sleek, lemon-lime colored machine. He paces me at eighty; he turns his head to look at me through an opaque visor. I don't know what else to do, so I nod. He just keeps looking at me. Then he points at me for a long moment, yanks his bike up into a wheelie, and rides it for several seconds before dropping back down. He levels his finger at me again and then they slice off into the western night at what must be one hundred and ten, given how quickly they vanish from the reach of my headlights, and then from sight.

The physics of it are quite nearly superhuman: a wheelie on a dark and icy freeway at eighty miles per hour. My passengers continue to snore so I look at Kaya for confirmation—she looks back at me for more jerky. At moments I've wondered if that cat on the motorcycle wasn't a phantom messenger, sent to hurry me back to Serala. Sent to tell me of the urgency.

THIS IS HOW IT HAS come to look in my head:

She is leaving Seattle the same day I get back. The only image that remains vivid is her crying as she slams Desert Storm's trunk, in which she can now fit everything she owns. The John Spencer Blues Explosion is blasting, absurdly, through her shot speakers. Her sunglasses are so big that I can't see any evidence of her tears. She's waiting on me now, to get through whatever I need to say. I grab her close and try some bastard cheerfulness, talk to her about the therapy of the road, but she's not really having it. She's nodding to get through the moment, but my words don't mean any more to her than the Pall Mall smoke merging with the slate Seattle sky. I begin probably my fifth sentence of the afternoon with a soothing *Hey*, the forthcoming *it's not so bad* or *it'll be okay* implied in the tone, a soft squeeze on her shoulder. But this time she interrupts me, seizes my forearm, and squeezes back.

It's okay, Eli, you don't have to do this—you don't have to say anything else. Then, quieter, *Please, don't say anything else.*

I am relieved that she's moving home to Connecticut. I suppose I fed myself the litany of lies that were opportune: she needed her family, needed to be "home," back nearer the one psychiatrist she trusted. She needed a road trip; she needed a fresh start. But it wasn't really about her, it was about me and what *I* needed that winter: to have her off my conscience.

I was so young and selfish that I didn't even understand that a decision had been made.

THE VELOCITY OF HER DESCENT during those months was shocking; it was both tempting and terrifying to imagine that my absence was part of it. But I was certainly not the lone factor—there were other forces at work, and this era was the first time that I saw that clearly, however irrational it was. The death of the strange dog in her arms and the attack by the frat boy alone did not evidence some occult magnetism of darkness, even given that they occurred in the same stretch of sidewalk, one day apart. But when one totaled the number of tragedies and traumas that had befallen Serala over her life, the sum was unnerving. There was no doubt that she summoned much of her misfortune by way of addiction and the situations that ensnared her as a result, but there was also this specter of violence and tragedy that seemed to stalk her, that seemed to stack evidence in her corner that the world was full of bloodletting in the shadows and people inherently cowardly and hungry for your pain. The good times we sucked down in northern California like wine were a bulwark and I was glad for them—I still am—but they were further evidence of the unwieldy responsibility I'd grown rapidly into the past summer.

The round that I fought with Jay on the porch of my house drew a line in the sand for me and I didn't see it till I'd stepped to Serala's side of it. I couldn't make him or anyone else understand the sanity and courage—if also the weight—I found in her filterless vision: looking squarely at the world, with no ability or inclination to turn away, to disown it, to smile at easy and fake distractions in all their ubiquity. Not to mention the other side of this coin: all the laughter that shook us, sometimes at the darkest moments, nor the fan of light that spread in my chest when I knew I was to be with her soon. The joy that she meant to me.

But my knight-in-shining-armor jaunt up north to try to keep her from self-destruction had produced an unwelcome precedent: for the first time, she'd turned on me. In the pit of wrathful despair I found her in, there was no room for love and affection, even for me. Despite that, I was there. And yet she'd accused me of selfishness: *You're here for your fucking self.* The worst part, of course, was that she was at least partly right. Of course I wanted to help, soothe, even save Serala, but ultimately that trip wasn't really for her. I had to go into final exams with a clear conscience. I needed to tell myself I'd done what I could. I needed to wrap her in my arms and hope right in her face: *everything will get better.* Consciously, I was a long way from realizing this—at the time I attributed her swipe at me to the lunacy of her blues. But silently it festered in me, another shred of selfishness in this world that she loathed and seemed to loathe her, and in this case it was mine to own.

At the conclusion of the street protests, the amalgamated progressive forces had been reasonably able to claim that we— *justice*—had triumphed, at least momentarily. But she didn't care to see that victory as a possible presage to change in the world's balance. I chalked it up to her rote pessimism and sucked hard on the consolation of her pride in me. I didn't hear the subtext, which was a common error of mine: *I do not belong amid hope—you have to do it yourself.*

Eleven

SHE CALLS EARLY ON A snowy morning a few days after Christmas. I'm sleeping off another night of trying to relive high school.

Hello?

Eli.

Yeah.

I tried to die, I don't want to live anymore so I took two whole bottles of the sleeping pills because I don't want to live anymore, I'm too tired—but it's not going to work.

I slump to the floor, thinking that I've got some very quick work to do here. But then she says:

My momma, she's making me go to the hospital, but I wanted to call you and tell you. I have to go.

The tears and the hysteria that rip her voice then are those of a child. She is enraged at not getting her way, after being patient for so long. And her momma gets on the line and says very calmly:

Eli, I'm taking her now. We have to go. We'll talk to you soon.

I can see her mother then, the blank in her lovely face: emotions so tangled and extreme that they cannot be held in an expression. I can see her facing Serala like she might have when she was a child, refusing to go to school or to bed. I picture her taking Serala's hand and pulling her toward the front door, Serala's mind sharp enough despite the drugs to know that resistance is futile, that an ambulance will take her if she doesn't go willingly, her body lagging anyway. But she can't refuse to live, she can only choose to die—through this distinction flows a river of difference, she has now learned.

And me? I know that there is nothing to do. I know that it won't help to break anything. Besides, I find that I'm not the least bit angry, just sort of wrecked inside. So I climb back into bed and pack pillows over my head and stare into their blackness and try to cry until sleep comes again—some sort of tribute to Serala, I guess.

To sleep, that is.

LATER, I'M DOWNSTAIRS IN MY mother's house, staring out at the rote drear of December Seattle: cold rain, early dark. I've got a pool cue in my fist, as if I've been practicing bank shots, but really it's just something to hold onto. I hear footfalls upstairs. Hugh appears, ankles first, through the slots in the winding oak staircase. His face is worried but bright, coming to care for me. He wears raindrops on his eyelashes, which at first I mistake for tears. Maybe the suggestion is too much, or maybe it has just finally become time, but I break then, drop the cue and cover my face. Hugh, wise to pain, sits me down.

The worst is over, E, Hugh is saying, kneeling in front of me, finding my eyes. *Whether she lives now or whether she does it for real*

*next time. Now you're ready; now you know you can't save her, you don't
have to. I didn't even try to save my brother; I didn't even know.*

I'm mute in the presence of Hugh's truth—and Hugh knows I
hear him, too, because, like Serala, he doesn't waste words much.
After a moment Hugh breaks the silence with a loud kiss on my
temple, his hold on my neck becoming a headlock, and we spill
our way into the shitty night on the hunt for catharsis.

THE NEXT DAY, WRITING OUT the last letter of the millennium to
Serala, I find myself thanking her: for all that she has given me,
all that she's spent trying to make my world more bearable, but
also for the lesson of pain, for the wisdom and the extra layers of
skin. In other words: much of it I might have written even if she
had succeeded.

I decided and signed off with this:

> *At any rate, you can take my unconditional love for you
> to the grave whether you swan dive into it tomorrow or
> trip into it in sixty years.*
>
> *My undying friendship, faith, respect, solidarity, and
> love,*
>
> *Eli*

The quantity of pills she took should have planted a bull
elephant in its grave. It wasn't just that she didn't die, she later told
me, but she didn't even fall asleep. I used to call her a superhero;
she used to call herself an alien. There were moments when mere

human physiology, however tested and re-molded by countless drugs did not explain her.

As illustration: one year before her attempt to die, on a weeknight in the Batcave, I come in late and she is weeping. The candles are burning and she is throwing her head back with a bottle of Merlot, swallowing duos and trios of sleeping pills. I am new enough to her to be very nervous, and might have dared to question her, but she offers wine and one pill to me and I am out before I know what's happened. The last thing I remember is her raw eyes on me and a smile that looks so contrary to everything else going on in her face. The first thing I see in the morning— nine hours later—is her sitting against the wall, still smoking, still drinking, still dressed in the same clothes, but now composed with makeup and sunglasses. Again she smiles and off we go for brunch.

But this was rote for her: the doctors came and went, sucked in and spat out by the revolving door of her blues. I liked to call her the Fidel Castro of patients: just as eleven concurrent U.S. presidents vowed to topple *el Papa* in their tenure, docs would approach Serala's case with confidence, even arrogance, sure they would be the one to let her sleep, to dull her pain. And after weeks or months they'd pronounce her bipolar (that catch-all), trying new scripts and following up with decreasing intensity. As she wrote to me in a goodnight message once:

> *i won't be able to fake it through another day if i don't lay down for a few—there are doctors to think about at 8 in the a.m. who need to be reassured. Pat one another on the back and see me well.*

The first time she mentioned electroconvulsive therapy, I didn't get it. I couldn't help but see it in my Hollywood-tainted renderings: Serala writhing on a table, wrapped in a blue electrical charge like a blow from a sorcerer's staff, eyes bulging like they did in her worst night terrors, her perfect teeth grinding right through the pad strapped into her jaw, a hint of sick smoke in the sterile air. An image to torture myself with, as if in solidarity, just like I suffered invented snapshots of her under the power of sick and violent men.

She just said it made her feel a little slow the next day, a little unsure of how she got home—not unlike a fifth of whisky might.

> *It's hell and medieval and frightening. It hurts, you forget everything, and it . . . deeply changes something inside. If it changes the part that makes me sad is questionable. i don't believe that it is as safe as they think because they don't exactly know how it works. But i do know . . . that it makes everything different. i used to run away . . . for things to be so drastically different, so i could try to see differently. i used to write to do it too. And i think that when i'm in a bad way, the idea is to just force something to shift, instead of being stuck in that bad place . . . lots of people think that it makes them worse, but less able to process the depth of the emotion they feel, which is why they hate it and why it appears to the docs that it works.*

No success except for whatever both she and the doctors pretended. She was the sweet anomaly, the challenger and the victor, the sad girl floating free of diagnoses, shredding professional guesses, getting by with the speed and barbiturates they prescribed, or by her own measured doses of coke and smack. Getting by with wine, sex, and sometimes love, enduring batteries of tests, no longer expecting the solution to be found in this world. She claimed to have tried it all: prayer, meditation, exercise, diets, hypnosis, acupuncture—to say nothing of the psychoanalysis, psychotropics, sedatives, the catharsis of poetry and filmmaking. She said that for a while she hoped a little, she had the juice for test runs of just about any Holy Grail. When her heart sank away, she indulged the myriad attempts—even the ECT—that the hope of others still subjected her to. Caring all the while for any number of fucked-up loved ones, including me.

Sleeping a few hours a week.

Hugh had claimed the worst was over because I'd tried; with good reason, Hugh believed that. His brother had never revealed to him what was probable the way that Serala had to me. Any shrink would have said Serala was crying for help and any reasonable person would have said I tried to provide it. Of course there are troughs in my heart where the question even now lurks like a vapor cloud: did I fail her? Was it selfish to watch her drive away to Connecticut? There are no pristine truths, of course. I did fail her and there was also no way I could succeed. What might be called irony, but which I count as a great blessing, is that we both failed: me in my rhetorical attempts to prop her sagging bones up against the world, and her in her attempt to put an end to it. Because much of my tension, guilt, exasperation, and fear were erased on the frozen white slate of that winter by her hand. She had presented me unequivocally with the impossibility of saving her and so I was finally free to love her.

But the worst was far from over.

Twelve

WHILE I SPENT A NERVOUS New Year's Eve with a gaggle of friends in the mountains, snowball battling around a massive bonfire, wondering if the specter of Y2K was ripping anarchic holes in the world, Serala sat in the psychiatric ward of a Connecticut hospital. I got her on the pay phone they provided once an hour.

You think you can do it? I ask her, inanely, incapable of the toss-off humor I know she probably needs. Serala sighs or exhales smoke—sounds the same.

I couldn't, Eli, that's why I'm here. Do you think I'd have done this to my momma if I could have helped it? Do you think I'm that awful? Her tone is edgy and she's treating me like I'm stupid. Although it was a stupid question, I don't appreciate it—I haven't thrown any guilt at her. She seems to realize this. *I can do it. Okay? Now I have to. There's no choice—I'm living like a fugitive now, I know. Gotta be good. Get off early with good behavior.*

Yeah, I say. *Good luck being good.* And I earn a small laugh, which relieves me. A schizophrenic, going berserk, hurls a chair across the room, apparently not missing her by much, but her tone doesn't reflect this as she reports it. Then there's silence, except for the general lunacy of the ward at war behind her.

Eli, how do you unchoose to die?

Before I have to answer, she is called to take her medication.

IN THE FIRST DAYS OF the millennium, finding the world disappointingly unscathed, I had to assume that the Department of Corrections' computer systems were up and humming. My small-town lawyer had been telling me for months: *Best case scenario, Eli, you plead to the marijuana and don't even have to show up here. Worst case, you gotta come out here and they'll hit you with a fine, time served, and lax probation.* But when I called him the afternoon of January 2, he didn't know what to say, because *it seems like they're gonna push the felony* and I had better head over in the morning. I was caught up in state politics: the residents of Grant County—which hosts the Gorge Amphitheatre—were fed up with city kids traipsing through for shows. They put pressure on the sheriff and prosecutor, both of whom happened to be running for reelection, to be hard. Hence the unheard of: pinning a felony on a kid for a half-dose of fungus.

The night before trial, I stood on the frozen porch of my mother's mountain house and looked out at the wide meadow multiplying and spreading the moon glow, as light as early dusk. I put on the Eagles' *Hotel California*, because it was the only cassette I could find in the dusty, disordered old house. I shivered, smoked, and drank two beers, telling myself I could handle whatever was coming if Serala could handle the return to her life. I thought about how, in a matter of twelve hours, we might both be locked up, fiercely lonesome in that way that only crowded jails and hospitals can make you.

THE LAZY LAWYER TELLS ME that if I fight the felony and lose, I'm looking at two or three months, plus serious probation, fines, and service when I get out. If I plead, I might get time served plus the same trimmings. When I ask the fat man through my clenched teeth what my chances are, he says

Oh, 'bout fifty-fifty.

I cop to the railroading job, and walk out of that courthouse a felon. It is the same day that Serala gets transferred home, back to the scene of her crime.

I see her standing gaunt and quiet in the doorway to her bedroom, the plastic hospital bracelet still looped on her tiny wrist, her skin dry and ashy, and hair heavy with grease. The linoleum of the floor is so clean it shines, nothing to suggest a warm corpse staring up at the doorway as hers would have at her mother. Maybe she catches sight of her reflection in the window over her bed and sees that her mother is behind her, in the kitchen, watching. Maybe Serala imagines the cold metal in her mother's guts, the panic she has put there. Maybe she turns, catches her mother's eyes looking. Maybe Serala smiles as wide as she can before she turns away, to cheer her mom a little, to suggest the course that she knows she has to be on now: the up-and-up. Or maybe not. Maybe she just staggers to her bed and lies stiffly, like a corpse.

THE NEXT DAY, I EASE my way down Stevens Pass through a wicked blizzard. I'm bound for the hospital where my father lies recuperating after his final major spinal surgery—to remove hardware screwed into his partially severed backbone. When I arrive he's already arguing painkillers with the doctor. The harried physician puts the prescription in my hands and tells me *not to respond to pressure from my dad.*

I hold that position for less than a day. My father is in a fit about how few OxyContins he's been given. He spends a long afternoon haggling with his primary doctor over the phone. He has enough to zipper his agony—not to mention his mind—for weeks, but that's not enough security for him. I acquiesce, but not without some resentment.

When I throw out a snide remark concerning a mishap with his über-complex entertainment system, he snaps. We have it out like never before, even in the most dire of times: when he caught me lying and drug dealing at fifteen; when he married a horrible woman and let her run roughshod over his relationship with me and Luke. I'm pouring out all the nasty alterations in his personality, how "*everyone* is alarmed," he's fighting back with all the defensiveness and denial he's not yet had reason to use against me. I unload the details of his addiction: the nodding off in restaurants, the slips in and out of reality, the weaving into the opposite lane driving, the stack of books that he's "reading" but truly hasn't yet started. He perches on the edge of the sofa, fitfully rearranging his agonized body, firing back with everything he has: that I don't understand a goddamn thing about it, that I'm selfish, that I'm trying to love him conditionally just like everyone else, that I don't respect him, that if I really knew how hard it was I'd be impressed that there was still a full clip in Grandpa's service revolver. And it's in that dark living room, beneath the wall of DVDs and vinyl, where Serala and he and I had felt easy with each other, working our way through old movies, that it hits me: *I have to love him precisely like I love her.* He's telling me that I should be proud that he hasn't ended his life; he's hinting that he might soon. He's telling me that I love him conditionally, like everyone else, that I judge him for the taking the only solution to his suffering.

It doesn't end in a long, firm, father/son embrace, sobbing, and pledging to fight through to some solution. He doesn't promise to quit and I don't promise to stand by his side. It doesn't end that way at all. I leave him there, curled on his bed, the pills and pistol in reach, an impossible distance in his eyes. I leave him there alone and partially helpless, in pain, depressed, and crippled, and addicted. I leave him there in unspeakable shame. I leave him there to go get drunk, carrying the same in me.

SERALA IS HOME AND HER family has no intention of letting her go far, not only out of fear but also because she is needed. In a compromise, she moves to Brooklyn and in no time at all, she is toiling hard at her father's advertising agency, leapfrogging by nepotism to near the top of the pyramid. Instantly capable, she earns the respect—and, in some cases, the fear—of everyone she deals with, from the office workers to big-shot clients. I imagine her swinging into this world with a yawn, writing computer programs and negotiating contracts like she's been doing it for years—instead of writing poems and making films.

IT IS ALREADY DEEP INTO March when she tells me she's coming out to Riverside for a weekend. Both of us are hoping we can turn the clock back, trick ourselves back to the better times in the Batcave, to the shiny promise of the American road ahead. But it's not that simple, of course, and there is a weariness to her visit, a slightly frayed quality, like our idea of how it should be has cycled too many times in our heads.

I think I tried to be the same. But when we returned to the Five Star, that formerly glorious dive, it felt dirtier, sicker—the reality dwarfing the charm. As the boozehounds and desperately drunk college kids swelled, we leaned into one another at the sticky counter.

Fuckin' place is ruined, Serala says, and drops her Pall Mall to the floor when an ashtray doesn't present itself immediately. She lights another and catches my sideways look and forces a smile. Nothing has changed about the Five Star and she knows that.

I bet you're glad as hell to be through with this place, huh? I ask, nodding out the windows to the smoggy sprawl and dying palms. But she just shrugs and points at her tumbler for another shot.

Only if by "this place" you mean the world, love.

And back goes the shot with a chaser of melodrama.

When we got in bed hours later and she moved close to me, the nausea I felt was not at her. It was at the image of waking up with her corpse. When I vomited it was not so much the booze and not at all her: it was her death come early to my chest in a half-dream born of whisky and dread.

She left early, as put off by me as by this whole world she had left behind. I watched her walk to a cab, only flipping a casual wave in farewell. Right there beside my ache at watching her vanish was a feather of relief, brushing it over.

I DIDN'T SPEAK TO MY brother Luke but once between September 1999 and May 2000. The exception was when I heard through our mother that one of his friends had died in the street, veins blown out by heroin. I'd gotten this news before Luke. But not much— he heard a rumor of it and called me from some point south and I told him it was true. He wept and I said nothing, because I can't go from angry words to words that have to be gentle enough for that. Instead, I told him I loved him and went and wrote a poem for that young, dead kid, who I'd spent some days with—a kid who had a bit of the same fetish for darkness as Serala.

When Luke appears on my front porch one night in early May and Kaya catches his scent and does one of her wild, charming freak-outs, we laugh. The freeway sings with Friday night in the distance and a Santa Ana gust shivers my brother's long, unkempt hair. The months of travel through Nicaragua, Costa Rica, and then Europe show not only in the wind and the sun treatment on his high cheekbones, but also in his eyes. In the way he looks at me is his alteration, and simultaneously the way I look back at him is changed. There's an open kindness I've never seen him aim at me. His presence says more than his words could: let's leave the trouble behind and know each other new.

You are shitty at keeping in touch and a mean big brother, he says.

You are a spoiled, self-righteous little druggie, I reply.

And he hugs me hard, like a man and not the kid I'd feared was in over his head, and I know that all of the conflict has indeed been squashed. Serala had counseled me once that sometimes you have to just *let shit drop.* At the time I'd said something about not sweeping things under the rug. She'd just shook her head, done explaining. That was the point: no explaining.

A wild and happy week of graduation hysteria followed, concluding with a nostalgia-driven affair between Mona and I, just in time for me to drive the golden coast north, home, away from her. I wound my truck through the spaghetti curves on the cliffs above the crashing California shore and sang along with Serala's mix tapes, belting lyrics out the window until Kaya, sitting shotgun, barked along with me. I stopped on deserted beaches and helped Kaya chase great, whirling clouds of seagulls up, against the sun, as if we were the wind.

Thirteen

IN JUNE, SERALA FINDS A lull in her hectic corporate schedule and catches a flight out. I was mired in the numerous projects of my mom's mountain home. It was she, Hugh, and me, and we were all glad of that.

The sum total of their previous time together was probably less than a month, comprised entirely by Hugh's rambles through Riverside in his fire-red Ford Rocket. They shared a wordless peace and comfort, and asked hungrily after one another when I was the intermediary. It was Hugh's brother's suicide that had brought Serala close to me the first day I met her, so it certainly pulled the two of them together.

We spent a lot of time kicked back in the fetid cabin, which was just down the road from the proper mountain "house." Hugh and I had turned it into a comfortable place: hand-carved easy chairs, ratty, soft old sofas, kerosene lamps, candles, and a hammock.

My father had given me Bob Dylan tickets for my birthday, so we headed off on a Saturday evening, back to the Gorge, despite my probation order to stay out of Grant County.

Dylan is opening for the leftover Grateful Dead. He plays some of my slow favorites—"Visions of Johanna," "Girl From the North Country," "Forever Young"—and we sit on the hill above the still-sparse crowd. He makes his rocking powerful; he is almost a young man, there, silhouetted against the bleeding sky on the lip of that canyon. When he strums and moves and bends double to blow through the harmonica, he commands healthy shadows, which slice across the dancing crowd.

When Dylan speeds it up and starts an energetic version of "House of the Rising Sun," Hugh and I run and tumble down the hill to dance barefoot, like the hippies around us. And when he rocks his way into "Tangled Up in Blue," I find there are tears leaking from my eyes and I feel better, higher than I have in as long as I can remember. I feel a part of Hugh and even a part of the dirty kids twirling around me, and a part of Dylan hunching over his guitar, jumping and strumming. When I look up at Serala, watching us from the hillside, above, I know she is with me—I know that the residual numb that has pried us apart since the winter and her "accident," is done. And I know she is fighting a smile, disguising it with cigarettes. It's fair to say that during Dylan's set of my favorite songs, I permit myself the vice of hope for her once again, I let the ragged thing back into my heart because I have to, because I can't be so free in the embrace of that music if I don't.

When Dylan is done and the legions of Phish/Dead Heads rush forward like refugees on a relief convoy, we split. The cabin is waiting with wine in its lap.

I glance at a trio of sheriffs standing around their cars as we roll past, not recognizing any, luckily. When a black cat darts across the county road a few yards ahead, Hugh curses and skids to a halt next to an alfalfa field.

Fuck. He puts his hand through his hair once. His fleshy, stubbled face sags a little and there is fatigue in his light eyes. *Oh well.*

He starts to crank the wheel to U-turn. I grab his arm.

No, Hugh, it's okay, it's okay.

Hugh shakes me off. He knows my story of a crazy late night traffic stop that went badly just seconds after a black cat darted across the road. Between that and my current probation Hugh has apparently been converted to paranoia greater than my own. I argue with him anyway, not wanting to burn our time on the big detour loop to other highways. But Serala ends my protest.

Don't be stupid—no, no, shut up. What do you think? This is not a discussion.

As we turn back south, I realize that she doesn't even know the event that turned me—and Hugh—superstitious. But she doesn't need to. As we take the longer but more majestic ride back, driving directly into the finale of the high plain's sunset, the dregs of rose light fall through the glass. In the backseat, she hums with Tom Waits's melancholy. I think about what good friends both of them are to not even permit a discussion. And I think about how I sort of hope we might all end up in bed together tonight.

I FIND MYSELF WRITING AND slugging wine in the cabin the next afternoon. Serala's leaned against my shoulder, busy with her cigarettes and biting off the split ends off her hair. Hugh's outside banging his drum, I can see him through the dusty pane: muscled forearms blazing, a cigarette dangling from his lip, an angry, tight rhythm shivering the air. As her weight leans into me more and more by the moment, I'm dreaming that I feel contentment rising in her. She has, for the first time in a while, brought me peace with this visit. My *tough as nails* best friend seems to be standing tall again, as if there had never been any faltering or earnest attempt to ditch life. It feels so good.

So Serala flew back to her corporate life and I was still bumping along with my summer of manual labor and bad writing.

When she described more ECT and psychotropic drugs I responded with rants against the medical establishment, asinine lobbying about how she should refuse it. When she needed my stable presence at her back, I was a chattering dasher along the sidelines, sending her Albert Camus quotes and manifestos on how Nader was going to make the world better (*so, hey, if you can manage, don't die*).

Meanwhile, in an inverse world, she was doing what she could, and she was clear about it: sleeping with strangers, shooting and snorting (*like a horse and a cowgirl*), drinking a ton, hanging out late nights with a big-shot rapper and one of his trumpet players. She was living, she said quite clearly, out of spite. Humoring teams of doctors and running a business by day, living hard by night. I had the audacity to ask her in one of my diatribes to live *despite* instead of *in spite,* okay?

Come October, I moved into the basement of a friend's house in the city, got a construction gig, and began assembling portfolios of seriously flawed writing for grad school applications.

I got myself dismissed early from probation, which immediately caused me to plan to leave America in January with an old friend for a few months of adventure. Serala took in my bastard poems and was severe but kind; I have no doubt that the one poetry program that accepted me was because of her pen.

I'm okay, I get out of bed most every day. This is hard. It's just the time of year. It's only mentioned by saying look at how far you are, and that was just a rough period, and thank god it's not like that again. Around my birthday, it seemed like my parents were high, floating on a cloud, that i was still here. It's fucking gloating. But that's not what's hard. A whole year later and it looks like everything has changed, things are better. And really i am better, better at what is the question. What has not changed is what's important, what is not gone, what i wanted to end so much that i would give my life to make it stop. Images of being strapped down because i couldn't stop shaking and i was cold and i still don't sleep. And electro . . . you know. i guess to look over this year and see that so much has changed, that i am stronger, that i can pretend again, that i can stand always—on my own again. i still like to sit with my knees pulled up to my chest when i cry. i like to be alone. The boy who occasionally sleeps in my bed tells me that i cry and toss through the whole 45 minutes that i sleep.

But i am okay, i don't want anything, and what i need, i have. So let your mind rest when it comes to me, know that i'm tough, that i'll be alright. i won't break like that again, i'll be around when you need me, still cursing the years that pass, the daylight each morning and those fucking birds that follow me around, eager to set up nest in any tree that is close to my bedroom window. Eli, i know you're my friend, i miss you. And i would like to feel you sleep next to me again. There's really something so sweet and innocent about watching someone sleep, and feeling their breath. i don't mean watching someone sleep after having sex with them. i mean the way it feels to have a friend, next to you, so close in your bed that you can feel love moving in and out with breath. It's really pure and warm. i miss that—you sleep like a puppy.

Well, this message took a strange nostalgic turn. It's good. It doesn't hurt to think of these things. That's all for me. i'll talk to you soon.

I lobbed emails to Serala from the haunted streets of Nicaragua; the grimy heart of San Jose, Costa Rica; from the postcard calypso beaches of Panamanian islands; once again from the Old World heights of Mérida, Venezuela; from the overwhelming magic of Cuba; from the freezing, culture-shocked carnival streets of Amsterdam. I wrote from Paris, where I slept too much on the couch of an old friend, and thought of Serala's restlessness, and walked the drizzly streets feeling strange; from Spain where I spent only one night with a wickedly attractive Spanish friend of my brother's who damn near stole my heart (and now she has, but that's a story for another time); from drab, unremarkable days of London where Luke was living his raucous college life.

In the U.K., two plans were born that secured my passage back to real life.

One: got word that I'd been accepted to the MFA program at University of North Carolina Wilmington and that I'd been given a position as a graduate teaching assistant. Given that I had nothing resembling teaching experience, understood few conventions of grammar, and my BA was in International Relations, I was pleasantly shocked by this.

Two: Serala told me that she would give me a ride—a ride from JFK International Airport to Mona's house in Los Angeles. Mona's house: where I would finally "give it a try" with her, a proposition unduly sweetened by the exotic distances between us and the inevitable homesickness I suffer. If Serala had any misgivings about driving me three thousand miles to Mona's clutches, she didn't give any indication of it at the time.

I CLEAR CUSTOMS IN NEW York. They wave me through without so much as a glance at my passport, which is disappointing as I have so many stamps to show off. When I get to baggage claim, the May light slamming the white-tiled room, I wince into the glare and see Serala—and none other than Monty at her side. It was, of course, not dramatic; I knew that they were in the midst of a streaky affair. I think that he even hugged me, but I was relieved when we dropped him at the next terminal for an outbound flight. This time across the country was for us.

That afternoon we rode through Midtown, managing to get lost on the way to Brooklyn. We played our way through the music we'd both accumulated over the months. The virile sun dropped in a square through the sunroof and she didn't shut it as she usually would have. She even reached up and opened it wider, and I touched her cheek lightly for a moment. She leaned into my hand and looked up at me, then got nervous and screeched out of the terminal. We smoked and smiled, held hands, and did not talk much. There was so little that needed to be said. We both knew that my rambling across a third of the world and what I'd witnessed in the course of it made us closer. I felt the pleasant soaring that I'd felt the first time she touched me in a drab dorm five years before.

There were still three weeks to come until I closed the most massive loop of my life and returned to Seattle, but that afternoon my feeling was one of coming home, distinctly.

Fourteen

WE HIT INTERSTATE 95 IN her brand new Passat, which resembled a chic club: blue dashboard lights, glowing orange needles on the dials, tinted windows and leather seats, bass pounding under your thighs. We went south blindly. It was not until Chapel Hill, North Carolina that we stopped, found a restaurant, and tried to hash out a trajectory. Serala didn't care—she just wanted to drive. I was in the land of my mother's family and thinking I ought to pay respects, make a better connection since I would be moving nearby in the fall.

Inside the restaurant, I have my back to the front window and am devouring my first true American cheeseburger in months. She picks at hers with a fork, wheedling out little coils of ground beef from the raw center—she liked meat to be *still breathing, just wounded*. It takes me half my plate to notice that she is upset. Her eyes are roaming with anxiety. She is hunched forward, her shoulders tense and high, hiding her long neck. Her long fingers toy with the napkin, a soggy fry, a pack of smokes, silver bangles singing a chorus line on her wrist, until she gets exasperated with her own fidgeting and her hands disappear beneath the table. She shakes off my questions then asks:

Do you have some cash?

I say sure I do.

Give me a twenty, will you?

I hand it over and she says, *I'll be back*, and gets up, and pushes through the door, and I think: *Fuck. Not in the middle of Dixie.* But when I look over my shoulder she is sitting with a trembling black woman on a bus stop bench. She doesn't even speak—I just see her put the bill into the woman's hand and turn away. I don't say anything when she folds back into the chair and takes a bite of her burger. But she acts like I have.

She was going to be really sick soon, Eli. I can't just watch that.

I say something about how she'd probably just put cash in an abusive man's pocket. Serala shakes her head at me and withholds comment.

WE ROLL INTO ALBION, GEORGIA, too late to rouse my grandmother, so I pull up to the mansion above her home, the ancient monster that hasn't truly been a home to anyone for generations. It stands above floodlights that barely reach the eaves, the steam of humidity rising through the beams even at midnight, a cenotaph of southern gentry and textile bounty. The house always makes me wince, the manifestation of every shred of discomfort and guilt I've ever felt about my ancestors and kin; it is the looming symbol of everything my mother fled, dragging me at age three to the most distant point in the continental United States. And yet it is gorgeous, dignified, and mysterious, hosting some of my most magical childhood memories and standing as a symbol to the rest of my family of smarts, work ethic, and success.

We roam through the dozens of rooms, the massive joists groaning like the song of whales, past the freeze-frame antiquity maintained since the house found a place on the National Historic Register. We drink our way through a half rack of Michelob, pulling eighteenth-century poetry books from dusty shelves, sitting silently on ornate cherrywood benches, looking around at creepy portraits of long-dead relatives. When I start to feel crowded by the haunts, she kisses me hard, my spine pressed against the huge, framed letter of Confederate secession. The phantoms' presence is dispelled and I drag her up to some master bedroom.

The next morning we sheepishly slide into my grandmother's cluttered house and she is *up and at 'em*, as they say, in jeans, bandanna, and boots, cheeks leathered and wrinkled. She has already been riding and grooming horses, plus an untold number of other tasks. But she welcomes us warmly and doesn't blink at Serala's dark skin, lip ring, and sunglasses. I breathe relief.

The shafts of Georgia morning light make me wince, and I am suddenly returned to a place I've been many times: an odd sort of awkwardness with my relatives. Grandma scorches bacon for me, leaves it half raw for Serala, pours water over instant grits and makes us full. I am surprised by how comfortable the two of them are together, how the edge that powerful women share transcends culture. Grandma as southern and white as they come, in her late seventies, with eight children, dozens of grandkids, a horse ranch and estate. She is gritty in her perpetual uniform of outdoor labor, and a veritable empire of the rural South still rests under her hand.

Serala, childless and unmarried, twenty-two, Yankee and Indian, carefully composed with perfume, designer clothes, and makeup, an entire Connecticut workforce under her hand.

A half hour later, in the dust and dander storm of tethered horses, to my shock, Grandma kisses Serala's cheek goodbye. I guess that they understood something about each other in that way that isn't mine to have. They were both, to be sure, always tough as nails.

We smoked stale weed that I'd squirreled away years before then shot off for Tennessee. Serala pushed a pill on me, and I went out like a rookie fighter, sinking through Lyle Lovett's crooning. And when I opened my eyes again, we were exiting I-40 into the blue dawn of that blue town, Memphis. We got lost, as was typical of us, making loops through the wakening ghettoes till we spotted a trashy motel. We pulled in and I went down for more sleep while she watched the mini-skyline through dirty windows and smoked.

We'd come for Graceland.

I was less than thrilled to enter the King's abode, but I knew it meant a lot to Serala, what with her odd obsession with the culture-thieving son of a bitch (I can't help it). I was hoping that I'd catch a better notion of what it was she dug so much about the so-called King. She'd watch hours of those garbage movies he starred in, and I'd seen her face open with pleasure when she came across his crooning on some radio station—she'd slap the dashboard—*fuck yeah!*—and light a smoke and sing along. She'd damn near broken my fingers once when, surfing the dial, I went on past "Heartbreak Hotel," forgetting the sanctity. And I'd asked her once what it was about him, but she'd just looked at me like I was a fool and said, *He died high as fuck, on the toilet! That's awesome!* and let it drop, so I had too.

When we get in line and an entire tour bus of ancient Long Island Jews files up at our backs, screaming at one another, tweaking their hearing aids with pale arms, I sincerely want to flee. But the fact that this makes Serala giggly and not homicidal is proof to me that she is happy. That it is enough to hold my arm and wait for a peek at the Jungle Room.

Later, we hit Beale Street. We sit in a smoky, plank-floored joint called the King's Table, where the waitresses are plump and quick and the fat black cook comes out to rub his belly and survey his domain. Blues crackle through the wall from a bar that is thumping in the dusk. We order a platter of meat: five different kinds, and slowly turn it into bones.

I tell her how the South seems more genuine to me in some ways, how people, in terms of their habits, their pleasures, their work, cut to the chase. There is no ceremony at the King's Table, no host, not even tablecloths, but the food they bring us is prepared to perfection. There are no high-cover-charge clubs with suited bouncers approving your attire; just dark and smoke-filled joints that don't hide that they are dens of vice. The bartender is warm but direct, no pretension that he is there to chat. He slides whiskies at us like it's sport.

I think I could live here, she says, and it sticks with me because I've never heard that before. *It's just run-down and blue enough. Just enough honesty to get by with.*

And as the music gets too loud to talk, and I watch her lean back and nod to the blues, smirk a whisky-smirk as an old man starts a guttural, lamenting tune next door, cock her head to the side, and blow a smoke ring that lingers just as long as it takes her to kill her drink. I can visualize her as a regular here. I can see her in a gracious mood, maybe high, maybe uncommonly rested, maybe with the afterglow of sex, waltz in and make witty chat with the fat cook, retire to her regular table, and wait for her platter of meat. And I can also see her angry, sleepless, or worse, marching down the muted glory of this street, stomping into the King's Table to drink it away, and everyone there allowing her to do just that without violating her with an inanity. And I can imagine her finding more than one of the kind of men she likes best (*guitar, dog, and pickup truck,* she says) in the ample shadows over the years.

The whisky in us is starting to burn and we move toward the music next door. It is a weeknight and the town is slow and easy. We match it with a lack of ambition, content to sit on high stools, listening to loud blues, and hold plastic cups of Maker's Mark. Serala gets tipsy and makes me do writing exercises for an hour before we can go back to the motel room with a bottle and cut as loose as we desire.

I don't quite recall where and when we buy the black hair dye. I only remember that when my scalp starts to burn and I am halfway into the bathtub and I try to stand up, she screams at me through her laughter.

No! No! Fucker! You have to stay there—stay there!

I have this photo from that night, just one: she's sitting on the bed, right hand plastic-gloved and holding the tube of dye, left hand clutching a plastic cup of whisky. There are streaks of the dye on her jeans and a thick lock of hair has swung down over her right eye. She is looking down and laughing, the way she did when she really got going, and her perfect teeth are showing and it makes me smile, too, every time I see it.

It turns out to be a sloshy blur, predictably. But somehow the joy we feel that night, the fun we have, still burns inside of me, independent of memory. And I do recall what I'm sure is the end of the night: shaking my newly black hair aside and tackling her onto the bed like I might do to Hugh. But then we roll over one time and though it isn't my intention, we go drunkenly fluid, and it becomes something I would not do with Hugh.

WE MADE IT TO SAN Diego two days later in time for dinner with an old friend of hers, which was overshadowed by the fact that we would part the next day in Riverside. Serala made comments about sticking around L.A. for a while with artist friends, maybe bouncing back and forth between the city and Riverside—maybe even getting to know Mona a little. And I said *yeah, sure, great,* but I didn't mean it because I knew she didn't either.

In the morning, in a sad Travelodge under an uncharacteristically dark California sky, I'm trying to pack, but she yanks me down on the bed. She's violent and hard and all through it I know that I will be with Mona that night—Mona, who is under the impression I'm officially "with" her now, despite the hedonistic months I've spent away. And I know how bad this is, but it's as if Serala's responding to those thoughts, *yes, this is bad, so fucking bad, you love it.* And when we're gaspingly done and drained, lying a foot apart on the bed, she puts her finger on my shoulder and says:

Oops. Fuck.

And I scurry to the bathroom and see the red crescent blooming on my skin and I'm not quite mad at her, but I do wonder. Did she do it to sabotage me? Did she do it to stake her claim that she came first and it would always have to be that way? Did she really lose herself? And I'm soaping the wound up, trying to wash it away like she does with her scars. It doesn't look too bad and I walk out shaking my head at her and she's dressed and sunglassed and smoking by the window and she says:

Sorry. Hey, let's go get me a dog.

DEATH ROW AT THE SAN Diego pound is a difficult place. All the mutts are barking and whining, those with hound genes baying, low and horrible, and they're all lying on concrete with shit everywhere, and big ceramic bowls of murky water, and that's it. We walk the gauntlet and a new keening goes up with every cell we pass. But Serala seems mostly unfazed. She has her eye, quickly, on a huge mastiff mix named Barney, who sits regally and pretends, unlike the others, that he doesn't give a shit. He's an easy one hundred and ten pounds and his info sheet says he has slight "behavioral problems," and that he doesn't do well with children or other pets. And so, of course, she loves him. But she's swayed by my argument that her car, her apartment, her neighborhood, her life, are too small for Barney. And besides there's this strange little red dog that has been looking at her in silence, stuck between two unruly Labradors, ever since we walked in. We go to her and she's not wagging her tail, because she doesn't have one I suppose, but it seems more like she's saying, *What the fuck would I have to wag about?* The way she looks up at Serala would not be called puppy dog eyes. It might be called *get me the fuck out of here* eyes, and after she looks into them for a while and I note that she looks like Santa's Little Helper from *The Simpsons*, Serala gives in.

Knox, as she immediately names her, rides in my lap for a while, but then we switch drivers so Serala can hold her. Trying to hurry through my doubts and the coming pain of saying goodbye, I swing the fancy car in and out of lanes, weaving through commuter traffic at a hundred miles per hour, letting music blast us and holding Serala's knee.

Mona's Ford is in the driveway and the lights are on inside the bungalow. Knox is like a nervous little forest creature on the leash, high stepping on and off the curb with wide eyes. In the last couple of minutes before I go knock and Serala climbs into the Passat, she is looking at the blurry moon in the dirty sky, the sweep of headlights on Indian Boulevard, down at her new dog, but not much at my face. I try to speak all the shards of thoughts floating around in my head. I think she's afraid of breaking down and I understand because if it weren't for the allure of this new girl and all my big plans, I'd be undone, too, at the hollowness opening in me as we disengage. In fact, we wouldn't be saying goodbye at all. But for now it's one-sided; I'm both selfish and helpless, and she knows it so she sucks in a sigh and forces a smile. But there is something left, I'm sure, to do or to say, besides to hug and make the broken, whispered promise, *I'll see you soon?*

I WAS COWARDLY: MONA WAS a bulwark between Serala and me just as Serala was a bulwark between Mona and me. Even before it began, I knew that Mona wasn't right for me—it was a boring redux of affairs I'd bumbled into before. As long as I was "honest" that I didn't intend anything *too* long-term, I wouldn't have to face either my own issues about commitment or the highly problematic element that my relationship with my best friend would introduce into any romantic scenario. I wasn't any closer to falling in a traditional way for Serala, but I was a long way from tranquility at the prospect of her self-destruction. I was less exuberant about walking through Mona's door than I would have been about staying in Serala's passenger seat, but I hedged and measured, and played it safe in a half-assed way. I told people who cared that my peace with Serala had come with the unsuccessful execution of her death wish, but the truth was that the whole schema was resetting in my heart as the years wore on. I knew that if I were a sincerely free agent, without a scholarship to graduate school and the obstacle of a relationship to a beautiful, exotic woman to insulate me, I might slip back beneath the stale and fruitless burden of being Serala's keeper and the failure that might imply. On the other hand, Serala's new life—her fancy Brooklyn brownstone, her corporate advertising job, her shrewd and knife-sharp business sense—was enough to cause me, at least subconsciously, to think that maybe she'd found a context in which she could manage. I wasn't quite so naïve as to think that heroin and its attendant dangers was going to be left behind along with poetry, filmmaking, and liberal arts, but there was always a plenitude of gray area and when I see myself inhaling the doses of her that I did, I think I must have only allowed myself to do because I was hoping again. The way she smiled and dreamed a little in Memphis, the absurd fun that we had on the road, the work ethic she exercised via cell phone with big-shot clients as well as employees that were remiss in their duties all smacked of a weathered woman somewhat reluctantly settling into pleasure and business—into life.

None of this is to say Mona was incidental; she was far from it—my affection for her and attraction to her were real, but the height I allowed "us" to be elevated to was out of proportion to anything I deeply expected to honor. I will have to say now that it was partially out of a need to keep Serala in a straitjacket of my own design: a "best friendship" that slipped those bonds in many moments and in many manners. In short, it was nothing definable, and so nothing that could be questioned or attacked— or resolved.

Fifteen

LUKE AND I SHARE OUR birth date, four years separated.

That year we're in my father's living room with my father and Mona listening to the *White Album* when the June Thursday comes. Serala rings and I move to the balcony where I have a modicum of privacy and can watch the few Seattle stars with her while we chat. I miss her quite terribly though I've been rotten about expressing that in Mona's presence. As I crush out my cigarette, though, Mona starts throwing mean glances at me through the glass doors. Serala can tell. I'm beginning sentences with sighs and *so's* and *well's*, using a tone of finality. I imagine her on her fire escape, limbs drawn together inside a pashmina, hair loosed for the night and made hectic by the breeze, looking down to focus as she does during important phone calls. I see her knock her cigarette out against the wrought iron because it's too short now and she needs a new one. The embers fall, whirl, and hit the hot Brooklyn asphalt like a scatter-shot meteor finding the sea.

What's the deal? Just talk to me for a few minutes, will you?

When I manage to get off the line, somewhat poisoned by Serala's tone, Mona is cold. She crosses her arms out on the little balcony and puts her gaze resolutely on the skyline. My brother and father, intuiting, juggle light conversation to cover up the awkwardness. I close the glass doors and try for pretending.

Hey, baby. Want to spend some time alone with me pretty soon here?

I touch her shoulders but she shrugs off my hands, the muscles knotted tight.

No, why don't you just spend your night on the phone with Serala? I'm sure she's much more interesting than me, even though I'm right here, trying to celebrate with you.

SO MY RELATIONSHIP WITH MONA was wilting like the azaleas in coastal North Carolina before we even got there in late August and moved into a small house in a subdivision. Serala knew.

There are oceans between what i feel and what i know and you can't build bridges across oceans. i'll start with what i know: it's you. i know that if there wasn't something so beautiful and true about this girl you wouldn't be where you are. i know that she touches a part of you that is only hers. i mean, you didn't know it was there until her hands held it. And that part of you that's hers is sweet in a way that we don't have words for. i know this must be true. How i feel is quite different. i feel like i should be in my car right now, on my way down to get you. Not to save you, but just to give you a place

That i feel you need.

Meanwhile, Serala's magnetism of tragedy—or is it merely the spreading stain of smack in her life?—means she loses someone else I never knew: a girl named Lila.

Serala staggers into a Bronx ER with a fading girl looped in her skinny arms. The place is crowded but the urgency is bold and even injured criminals hop out of the way. I see Lila's head on Serala's shoulder, hungry just for the ultimate rest she thought she was getting, Serala cursing like a sailor as she hands her over with the facts: *junk, HIV positive, probably not a fucking accident,* all the while thinking how lucky Lila is. Wiped out by the effort of her delivery and sleeplessness, as Lila vanishes between double doors in a flutter of gowns, the world tilts on its axis and Serala faints onto the linoleum. They get busy with their assumptions and their paperwork, with their restraints and tranquilizers, and they hold her until her shrink can vouch to spring her, get her back to her impressive theater of getting by, her life where no one who loves her wants to hear about a junkie friend kicking the bucket, *no,* not now.

Not knowing, she says in an email, whether her tears are coming or going, she lets them just sit on her face as she writes me these headlines from her planet. *All in a weekend's work,* she says.

> *i'm no buddhist, but in some ways i have a sense of enlightened defeat. Because i don't feel like i have anything to fight, nor do i want to. The past few days have tested me beyond my reason, beyond my despair even. And then there was all the shit that i added. But now i think i'm past some of it, past being scared and alone, past lineless too, i think all the way to solitude.*

i wonder if some things i will consistently have to re-learn, and every time will i feel so stupid, remembering the last time that the lesson was taught? Or is it more hopeful than that, to teach me that nothing is real or true? That the lessons learned from heartbreak are not so much lessons as they are crutches. And just as the heartbreak seems cyclical and repetitive, it is proof that its opposite is too. Nothing new

i guess. Just reminded.

Eli, i'm sorry for laying my shit on you. i guess in moments i want to feel like something could make a difference. Like strength could somehow be gathered from sources outside myself, and that it could be held in words. But i think that for years i've been mistaking strength for survival. Survival is reflex, instinct, it can't be helped or controlled or even suppressed (i've tried). Strength is something that i think i still don't know anything about.

i'm glad you're closer, but 500 miles and 5,000 miles have little to do with being close . . . the heat and humidity of the east coast right now make you feel like you're breathing with a plastic bag over your head.

Do you feel ready to be there? Are things okay? Or rather are you okay? And Kaya? And Mona? Road trips are usually good for working shit out, for me they have been, both alone and in relationships.

i love you Eli.

i miss you, a lot.

Tuesdays are my slow days. I'm awakened midmorning by a call from Mona at her new job, selling coffee in downtown Wilmington.

Wake up, turn on the news—some big catastrophe's happened in New York.

Sleeping in the shafts of Carolina sun is so sweet, that I doze again for a few minutes before hauling myself to the sofa. I twist the Venetian blinds open as I click the television on, so the horror erupts on the screen as the tranquil blades of light cut the room. My vision is swimming, and I fall back onto the scratchy sofa and hold my head in my hands as the first World Trade Center tower smokes and then buckles in real time, and Aaron Brown of CNN slowly turns damp eyes back at the camera, says quietly, *There are no words,* and drops his microphone.

My thoughts flew to Serala, but her first email that afternoon assured me her caustic survivalism was very much intact.

There's just too much going on right now, it's like a movie and aside from the worry about people i know, i'm not sure that i think it's so tragic. Maybe i should see that "freedom has been attacked," but i'm not worried because George W promised that my "freedom will be defended."

Serala was up there in the thick of it and more than a little bit brown-skinned. She admitted to being scared for her family because they certainly looked the same as Arabs to angry white people. She laughed it all off, of course, after copping to her anxiety. She described the short walk down the block for smokes in her Irish-American/Italian-American neighborhood: *No,*

*really, it's just funny: these fuckers see me coming and it's like "what do I
do? It's brown but it's got tits. Can I still punch it?"*

But after a few days, she allowed the images tumble out in
tentative fragments.

*Driving home from work, i couldn't take my eyes off
the thick smoke smoldering in place of the towers, nor
could i hold back tears. It seemed that no one could in
any of the cars around me. Envoys of dump trucks full of
buildings' debris roll past like a parade. And even though
we've had two incredibly clear, sunny days, from here
we can't see the sky. The wind changed directions today
so all the clouds of dust and smoke loom, it's like the sky
is expressing for us. Knox can't help but shake with fear
every time the sound of military jets disrupts the eerie
quiet of night. The city is silent except for the sounds of
trucks removing the wreckage. It's all so strange, everyone
is waiting. And aside from the racist violence, we are
wrapped together under this cloud, all careful not to
disturb the sorrow. There isn't even any kind of relief
effort to organize, hospitals are waiting too, quiet because
there is no one alive to treat. And it is a military state.
Hummers and jeeps are the majority of cars on the roads.
Check points everywhere.*

ANXIETY DISRUPTS MY EASY ROUTINE of books and lectures. The
need to be there with her swells so I buy a ticket, a month to the
day since the towers fell.

As the 747 banks a turn around Roosevelt Island and veers in, I can see the wreckage arching like bad postmodern art out of the skyline. It seems that smoke still rises from the rubble, but I'll later learn it's merely dust—composed of particles of bone, retina, skin, cartilage, and even the human heart as well as steel, concrete, glass. It's sent to orbit each time a dump truck rolls away with the gravelly ashes. Around me, all the passengers are white-faced and weeping, the plane a funereal spiral down to the tarmac.

But Serala does not need my urgency. She is calm, distant, and quite cold—not toward me specifically, just closed up. It is as if she's fought quite a battle to get her sails up in this storm, but now that she has, she's moving fast and strong over the swells, cutting a path straight away, harnessing the violence. After scooping me at the airport, she has to return to the office, and so I hop a train to survey the landscape myself, figuring that a writer should face it.

SAMAR IS IN THE CITY, trying to find a place for herself as a volunteer near Ground Zero. I convince her to meet us in the village. Over sushi and sake, I feel embarrassed at who I used to be, mortified that Serala saw Samar and me at our ugliest stage. But I feel wizened to be so far past that era, years down the road, with the fortune of having both of them at my side. Especially in contrast to the tragedy just blocks away, all of the old drama seems pale and wasted.

I find myself smiling over a urinal, thinking back to the night Samar and I finally split, the absurd confrontation in the bathroom at the house party. When I push back through the door, I stop and linger a moment, watching the two of them. They are leaning in over the sashimi, picking at it with chopsticks, eyes bright, smiles rising and falling on their faces. There's an unmistakable love between them—and I know now, in this moment, leaning on a doorjamb in a Manhattan Japanese joint, blocks from the wreckage of American innocence, from what this love arises: two of the toughest people I have ever known, women who have survived the best attempts of bad people to erase them. They hold their heads up, and cross their arms against the world, and they recognize it in one another and show due respect.

We need an antidote to the sadness of the city. To my surprise, Serala leads us to a Bulgarian disco, packed with Eastern Euro kids, all going wild with vodka, and cocaine, and loud outfits. Weeks before she'd said to me in a lighter moment that *you've never seen me with my dancing shoes on* and it's true. She, who usually trips on the stairs and often slams her hands in doors. I don't know if it's the need to dance off September 11, her unaccountable love of the Bulgarian house music, or the desire to surprise me, but she's something. I dance with her and Samar, and sweat a lot, and pretty soon it's 3 A.M.

Out in the cold street, I stumble out to the middle of the avenue to see an apricot moon dropping pearly light down through the dust. A group of soldiers stand in the shadows, blocking entrance to the avenue; they stamp feet and blow hands for warmth. A short gust comes through the night, and lifts the dust off the ground like a fog, and we get a train for Brooklyn.

I felt the first slivers of it coming the next day as Serala drove me to JFK: a blueness that engulfed my world for the next week. We sat on the filthy cement outside of ticketing holding hands.

I suppose I could chalk up the toxic feeling that entered me to witnessing the wake of 9/11. But somehow I don't think it was that simple. I spent days fantasizing darkly, sketching sinister shapes onto notebooks, and erasing more than writing. I told her, in an email soon thereafter, that I felt as if I'd blacked out and seen something or learned something that was so horrible it had poisoned me, but that I couldn't remember what it was. And she told me, wryly, *Welcome to my world.*

But, for me, the cage lifted somewhat soon, as it usually does.

I CAN'T HELP BUT IMAGINE the city then as a physical representation of her emotional landscape: the destruction, the terror, the militarization—the drugs, the shame, the doctors. Whether the scope of slaughter in New York City was going to forge the nail that punctured her cynicism and really send her spiraling or, rather, if it was going to simply harden her more and multiply her cynicism, I didn't know. I didn't want either to occur, I suppose, which is why I blindly flew north—as if I could have changed it. A lot of my rushes to Serala's side were, as I've said, for me. In earlier years I rode the hubris that I could somehow deflect pain from her or protect her from her own filterless eyes or the disturbances in her soul. By the time September 11 occurred, though, I was merely doing what I needed to for my own conscience. Sure, I could soothe her—or join her in self-soothing with dance, booze, and laughter—but I was pretty clear that when I retreated to North Carolina nothing would have changed for her given the astounding evidence of life's horror that was splayed across the landscape of New York.

Samar and I tried—me half-heartedly, Samar with some passion—to point out the heroism of New Yorkers to Serala, to suggest that human nature perhaps comes close to balance between the bloodlust of some and the selflessness of others. But she'd just cackle softly. *Right,* she'd say, *so you think the people who flew those planes wouldn't be "heroically" volunteering at Ground Zero if we'd attacked their country? And after seeing this, these selfless, "heroic" Americans would never support such a thing inflicted upon innocent civilians somewhere else, right?*

Of course, this was Serala in short: whereas this kind of philosophical debate would go well over a good wine and filet amid old university chums, Serala drained all the abstraction from it, because the answer could make all the difference.

Of course, we were already bombing Kabul.

Sixteen

It wasn't a week after I got back to Wilmington that Serala called in hysterics. I was sitting at my desk, fingers poised over some nascent essay, daydreaming out the window that framed a piece of my suburbia.

Why the fuck, why, Eli? Why if you say you love somebody would you hurt them? Why would you do fucking horrible things to them? How could you use your fucking hands against them? How?

I didn't try to coax the event out of her; I knew I couldn't, at least not that close in time. And I couldn't answer her questions, so I tried to soothe her with the insufficiency of *I love you's* and *I know's* and *I'm sorry's*. But after her tears dried, and I couldn't hear her sniffles anymore, and instead heard Springsteen's "Used Cars" faintly, and she started with small brushstrokes of self-restoration, *Got to get to work, everything in its place, suck it up, power through,* I allowed the call to end with a lame encouragement to *keep your head up*.

I could see her, driving—as I knew she had been by the wind

and horns in the background—with both hands uncommonly on the wheel, trying to compensate with proper posture for the fact that she can't even see the road through her tears. The window is cracked for the constant cigarette, and the wind sucks all her loose locks of hair toward it. Her eyeliner has run so much she's not even fighting it anymore, bound to hide in a bathroom along the turnpike somewhere to redraw her eyes before she gets to work. I imagine she's going uncharacteristically slow, needing every moment possible between her and the job, all the questions from her employees, the myriad needs from her father's office, the whole banal nightmare chugging along just as it was yesterday; it's both symbolic and real that yesterday never ended for her. I imagine that she left a dark house where no one was awake, where they were, in fact, more than asleep, in the heavy Nothing after a binge. I imagine she had lain for several hours with red lines weaving through her eyes as some sick man snored next to her, a hand on her shoulder in sleepy care, no memory in his cells of how he'd treated her, what he'd done because maybe just as dreaming is the inverse of living, his need in dream is inverted, too, is to care for someone, use his hands sweetly. But Serala without the consolation of sleep, without the possibility of calling it a nightmare, has known instead that it is her life, and the anvil of resignation has sat on her chest, next to his hand, through all the small hours. Maybe there is also the ebbing relief of smack running laps through her body, but I suspect it had run out hours ago by the way she'd been weeping.

And in mid-reel, I chop this footage: I shake my head and look out the window at my sunny subdivision, where fat southerners cut their rectangles of grass with riding mowers outside their one-story brick houses, and the mailman waves to them and I can see him whistling, all of it just a pantomime from where I sit, but good enough to yank me out of my best friend's world that morning. And then, I'm sure, I go back to work on an essay, or grade some English Composition paper, or watch the awful news with my taciturn girlfriend.

LATE THAT AUTUMN SERALA WRITES of her mother more honestly than she ever has.

> i . . . went to feel the comfort of her arms, her warmth.
> When i saw her, i couldn't speak, just cried. And she
> held me, like i wanted and cried too. And when her ring
> pressed into an almost healed scrape on my back i flinched
> and pulled away. She asked what happened, i sat down
> in the chair across from her, lit a cigarette, turned my face
> away and lied. With a forced smile, I giggled and said
> it was really stupid, something about Knox and tripping
> up the stairs, scraping my back against the banister. i
> wanted to scream at her, Eli. i wanted to yell and ask
> her how she could love me so much, look into my eyes
> and force me to keep living. i wanted to blame her for my
> life, not for my birth, but for not letting me go two years
> ago. i wanted her to walk into my room that morning and
> sit with me and let me go. Like mothers in the movies,
> when their children are dying of some terminal disease.
> To understand and let me go.

MOST TROUBLING AT THAT TIME, as the weather slogged into her worst part of the year, was that sleep became more elusive for her than it ever had been. But Serala had a bag of tricks to get her to dawn.

> . . . *nights i find my own arms bound tight around my knees gently rocking. Or sitting up with two or three crossword puzzles strewn about, alternating between them. Or just laying still, humming to music with Knox curled up closely, under one arm. Sometimes i drive all night, down to the back roads of Jersey, to the shore and back home, and i always stop in the same places, but that depends on how the moon and stars look. But probably once every two weeks or so, i catch the* NY *Times delivery truck driving down my street and i follow it, staying about half a block back. i go from stoop to stoop, removing one page from each paper, then carefully folding it and putting it back in the little blue bag.*

ON THE DARK BORDER BETWEEN autumn and winter, one of the few people to whom I'd gotten moderately close in my time in Wilmington, a big-eyed and beautiful girl, tried to die and failed. I was upset and I reached out to Serala, but when I did I realized I had set her off, probably done more damage and made the season even worse.

> *Your friend is fucked. From the second she opens those sad eyes, everything that seemed unbearable to live through before will be automatically and infinitely worse.*

And the truth of it is that we don't get any stronger,
we just become better liars. You don't believe your own
smile anymore. One thing that might be the same always
is that when you get to the point that you can actually
do it—or try—it's because you want nothing. And if
it doesn't work and you live, how do you un-make the
decision to die? Just because you live, how do you ever
"really" live after? When you stop wanting, when you
don't want to see another thing, when you don't want to
love or be loved, when you just don't "want" anymore;
how can you make yourself?

Over Christmas, Mona flew home to California and I flew home to Seattle and my father—Luke was somewhere between Mexico and Panama. After hearing of my plans, Serala reported with uncharacteristic obfuscation that she was coming to visit Cassie in Seattle. But it was me who picked her up at the airport.

She climbs in, bundled in her peacoat, and looks at me, I'm relieved: her eyes are different than they were in October and the wake of 9/11, and it isn't merely the green contacts. She seems open again. But I'm also unnerved: she looks so magnetic to me that keeping my boundaries in place is sure to be a challenge.

We eat Thai food on University Avenue, a few blocks from her one-time apartment. While green neon light bleeds through the window, we push around topics (October, heroin, Mona, and writing) like the scraps of napkin she's tearing up and arranging on the table.

What should we do with this old town for the next couple days? she asks, raising her eyebrows over the contacts, which is spellbinding really, which is why I look away as quick as she does, shrug. *I want to see your dad,* she says, *and not just in passing, but to really have some time.* I look at the creases in her hands that are folding and refolding her scarf now, feeling unaccountably embarrassed.

You should probably see him on your own, no? I ask, hoping vaguely that she will disagree, but she doesn't. She nods like it makes sense and I know it does. And then our food comes.

She's shy with me a little that night, like we are on a date, and that arouses me. But I swallow my spicy soup and take her for a chaste evening of goofing around with Louis and his rambunctious dog—a simple affair of old college friends, none of this overwrought struggle with mortality, loyalty, ethics, or love. I shared a bed with her that night, though. I sucked down slack-jawed rest like a glutton while she no doubt sat nearby and watched, then slipped off to Cassie's in the morning.

THE STATE SCHOOLS' SPRING BREAK fell in March and Mona and I headed for New Orleans for two days of wandering the Garden District and French Quarter, sampling Cajun dishes. The air hung like wet sheets and promised, already, that summer was coming. We strolled miles of Magazine Street and I slid into dark places for beers while she shopped in boutiques, the magic of the city enough to steal us from our own cycle of sniping misery.

And then my father called and told me it was time to put our dog Sky down. After fourteen years, cancer, the loss of a leg, arthritis, after thousands of miles of travel and many different homes, and holding the flame of our little three-man family like a hurricane lamp, she was finally done.

I sit at an outdoor café table, fight my tears with a cigarette—and lose. Mona faces me, her hands on my shoulders, until I let myself weep and then she does a little, too. She wants to share every shred of pain, wants to match me tear for tear, wants to give me her solidarity. The flipside of this desperate desire to enter me completely, to meld, is very unhealthy and damaging, but in this moment on a Cajun street with strangers all around, she's perfect. Finally, she pushes the salt from her eyes with a painted nail.

You have to go home, she says. *You'll regret it forever if you don't. Go.*

I KNOW THAT SERALA DID not take the death of a dog lightly. I know that she was with us when we gathered, lit candles, said our farewells, and the gentle vet shot Sky's mainline full of blue poison and she breathed once and grew cold. I know Serala said a prayer about peace for her and helped us send her on.

My father's first grateful email was sent before I even landed again in North Carolina. And more followed, along with phone calls. He was desperate with the need to make Luke and me know the value of our visit, and to make sure we believed his intuition that Sky was still lingering. But he didn't take this as a bad sign, only a signal that he had to let her know it was okay to move on. My father was not a new age flake; he was, in fact, a cynic. But he rushed headlong into vague spiritualism, talking to Sky, writing her letters, doing whatever his equivalent of prayer might have been. If it struck Luke and me as odd, we probably chalked it up to the giddiness he felt, also, at being finally free—of caring for Sky and free also of OxyContin's hammer, having pulled off a switch to a lesser narcotic. And, indeed, he quickly assembled plans to travel to Ecuador, a country that had called to him for some time.

The night before he left, just a month after Sky died, he called me to say goodbye. He was excited about the trip, but he felt angry with the many friends who, instead of supporting his plan to reenter the world, tried to warn him away from adventure. They cited cautions that ranged from state department reports to the weather.

I swear, Eli, it's like these people that allegedly love me would rather I stay in this goddamn house for the rest of my days and wait for their phone calls.

I empathized, but I was whipped by a twelve-hour day and I begged off the phone, wishing him well and making sure he knew that he had my support for his adventure.

If I'd been paying attention, I might have suspected what was coming. As it was I was uncharacteristically happy and oblivious on that Friday morning, April 12, 2002. I was eating crepes with Mona while the dogs tumbled around, the cat hunted lizards, and the news unrolled the story of the coup in Venezuela—*next door to my dad,* I thought, vaguely. Mona answered the phone. Then her brow furrowed. Then she turned white and handed over the receiver.

The consulate was formal, then almost tender. *Your father died of an apparent pulmonary embolism,* she said, *here in Quito this morning.*

Part III

Seventeen

I SAT IN A BEACHSIDE bar alone that night, pouring Coronas I didn't taste down my throat and thinking about my father's bills, his business, his mortgage, his body. A gaggle of logistical stand-ins for the rages and sadness that I was due.

Serala would know what I meant if I said "numb." She'd know that numb is not exactly right. She'd know it's more as if all the pain that's coming is bottled up, bound to wreak chaos in the future, but, at first, not unlike how a very stressful day feels.

Mona had broken at my side just the way she did a month before when news of Sky came. She sobbed till she gasped and held onto me like a castaway—her love went beyond comforting me and into her own wild grief. She had whispered and wailed her promise to do anything for Luke and me in the coming madness, but when I told her I was going alone to the beach in the dregs of the spring day, she had fought me bitterly.

I knew that Serala could tell me if I was losing my mind, if my heart was still inside—or if what this numb truly meant was that it had somehow slipped out of me while I was letting cigarette smoke crawl out of my mouth against the sunset. I called her from my truck, which at the time seemed a logical place to spend time, even parked. For some reason she was in Washington, DC.

Hey, I said.

Hey, love, she said.

I didn't say anything else, and she said:

Should I pull over?

She stayed calm and clear that day, on some sketchy DC side street, en route to Monty, or a score, or God knows what. She'd been paying attention when I'd reeled off the details over the last month: Sky lingering, my dad giddy, the warnings about him flying off into high altitudes with his damaged body. She had suspected what was coming; maybe she just wanted me to have a few more days intact.

Her words in the time that intervened between his death and his memorial were straight and so right at a moment when almost every sentence made me want to cut out my tongue.

> *i said i'm coming for you, but that's a lie.*
> *i am coming for*
> *a drink*
> *a smoke*
> *a big pain*
> *and a big love.*
> *I'm coming for a friend,*
> *to be a friend*
> *because i am your friend.*
> *And i am coming to give you a hug*

and hold you close
as if seconds can last a lifetime through.
i am coming
because i need.

It's true i knew him through you and with you, but separate from you, too. i thought of him, maybe in similar ways as you did, not as Eli's dad, but as a pained and wise friend. i thought of him as one of the only people i've ever met that could understand love and pain like me, probably more. i need . . . to come to Seattle to allow his passing to be just as real as his life. i think things about death and your father's that would probably break your heart, but i don't think that any of it . . . would be a surprise to you.

The evening of my father's memorial, I stall outside the building, taking little hits off a flask. I know they won't start without me and I don't want to start without Serala. It doesn't occur to me to be angry that she's late, just scared that she won't make it at all.

She and Jay round the bend and I watch them approach against the gunmetal sky. She's dressed in a black pantsuit, a black pashmina, black shades. Jay is buttoned up and has a flashy tie jumping on his chest as he strides. They're walking fast together, purposefully but comfortably, like a couple of lawyers or detectives might walk into a press conference. Serala removes her shades, and they both look into my eyes from a distance, and they're both strong enough not to weep and wise enough not to try to smile—

they just give me their eyes. It's another one of those moments for me, like Serala meeting my dad, like her and me and Samar in the sushi joint in the village—the conjuring of a broader notion of family, the warmth of being in the middle of a great bed in a bad fucking storm. Seeing her and Jay together, getting squeezed tight by both of them, having my hands on both of them at once—it almost makes me cry for the first and only time that day.

We almost started without you, I say with her face pressed to my neck.

No, you didn't, she says, and takes my hand and we go in.

Standing vertiginous at a podium in front of that sea of faces— memories reeling past in each one—I don't feel nervous, just incapable. I've spent days composing and revising my eulogy, to the point of striking and rewriting, striking and rewriting, the same adjective, drunk at 3 A.M. But it falls through me in that moment, the knowledge that words won't cut it, that there is no way to adequately honor my father there. But then I glimpse Serala: a small island of darkness. I can breathe then, and I punch through the blockage and read with passion if not clarity.

As the service ends Dylan sings "I Shall Be Released" from a boom box and the room lines up to light the dozens of candles on the altar. Luke and I set up a two-man gauntlet of tenderness at the door, to hug every person that comes through, to emblazon our smiles into all the weeping eyes.

That day wasn't for us or for our father, of course—it was for everybody else. All those people may have come thinking they were honoring our father, but they mainly came for closure. We provided it as best we could. We won't have the privilege of closure until God knows when—probably never. But it was a gift that only we could bestow on all the people who loved him—however inconsistently, conditionally, or poorly. That's why neither one of us wept that evening, even as sobs broke the crowd at their knees.

But Serala knew all this already; she was faintly angry, I think, with the arrangement, and she stood off to one side of us, staying near, as if to catch us if we fell.

That night was mad with rock 'n' roll and whisky, with furtive celebration and farewell, our house packed and bright and shaking with laughter and guitar, as my father would have wanted it. At one point, deep into the morning already, Luke and I cut ourselves from the thinning crowd and went into our father's office to play a song that we knew would break us. We needed to fall apart at least once before the ceremony could be complete and we invited Serala in but she refused. Instead she stood outside the door like sentry, arms crossed, warning away drunk friends.

I remember kissing her, once, not entirely chastely, and her smiling, telling me to behave. Eventually she disappeared with Cassie and the process ended with me, Samar, and Luke on the front porch, sharing the last drops of booze in the house—a Corona—and watching a new dawn build itself above the familiar trees.

SERALA AND I SEE EACH other only once more before she flies back to her life. It's in a Greek restaurant in Fremont, a stone's throw from the funeral home that burned my father's corpse. The sun is setting, and we are eating lentil soup, and she is probing gently, though with a spear of a gaze, to find out what I need—to find out if she should stay. The place is near empty and all my words sound too loud, wrong. The Greek waiters can't keep their eyes off her, though, and so they keep arriving at inopportune moments to top up water glasses and whatnot. She watches me, worried, waiting for me to betray something I've been hiding.

I don't know what we said, but I know I was still more or less stoic, still angry. I'm glad I have her words here, scrawled in her wild script and blue ink on a Hallmark card.

So if you find that you've gone too far and can't find your way back, if you find yourself too lost to find anything and are ready to be found, Eli, I will come for you. If you ever need me to—no matter where or what spaces have passed between us and places we have passed through, if you find yourself lost and lonely, I will find you. Always.

In June I faced my and Luke's birthday, our father's birthday, and Father's Day. A row of grievous dominoes like Serala had had in the winter. Things were all wrong in Seattle then and I should have shoved off early in the summer for New York, or Carolina, or any point between, found solitude and grieved without familiar eyes inevitably reining me in. But there was my father's "estate" to sort (he'd written a will years earlier when he had had some money), Mona and me to somehow resolve, and Luke to watch out for.

I might have tossed all those concerns to the wind and coasted to Serala's bed, but she was back in the stiff, corporate saddle. She never had much to say and everything she did say was clipped, impatient, bored. I deduced that employees lurked around, guilty and nervous, waiting for her to look up from her desk, just to ask her for small things; I deduced also that sometimes she snapped at them and set them scuttling away. I know that sometimes she went to great lengths to help one of them out of a jam of their own making. I understand that during business hours she sometimes closed her office door to weep. I heard that later, alone in the offices, she shut her office door to suck lines of smack through her thin nostril off the cluttered desktop. I know that the small relief that these practices brought her was usually enough—enough to get her on the road to Brooklyn where she could chain-smoke, blast her rocking tunes, and sometimes call me, talk sweet and low about how the road looked or where she would go if she only could.

But then, slipping off the ledge of the night into the oppression of another morning, it would all begin again.

> *The bank-regional vice president . . . yesterday in less than 45 min i got him to extend us a line of credit for 1.6 million dollars. We just got an 18 million dollar contract (6 mill. a year for the next three years) for a new product and we have to buy new computers, 30 of them, and hire more people. It's vaguely interesting . . . After all the pills or drinks or fuck or none or all, there is a whole day ahead, and work and lawyers and meetings. A desk, an office, business-financial statements, computer systems, pantyhose, and high-heeled shoes and the fucking sun . . .*

> *I've been in a rotten mood for the past three years.*

I was in a rotten mood, too. And I suspected I would be for at least three years. It's too easy to say that my grief over my father brought me closer to Serala, but it's also true. Though she clothed many of the causes in half-statements and cryptic commentary, grief underwrote the darkness of her vision, at least as much as heroin and whatever manifestation of mental illness she suffered. In fact there is an argument to make that Serala simply grieved: that's what was "wrong" with her. She grieved when her friend Lila died, when the mystery Original Lover died, when friends I never knew died, when her beloved childhood dog died, when that strange dog died in her arms on a Seattle street corner, but she also grieved over every single awful headline. When the rains took tens of thousands of shanty-dwelling Venezuelans to their deaths in 1999, my sorrow, even having lived there, paled beside hers. More complexly, she grieved when people hurt her—Monty with his infidelities, the violent frat boy she pepper-sprayed, or others, sick men with drugs to offer that I would still rather shank than consider.

Enlightened resignation to the impermanence of life and, therefore, suffering, is something that Buddhists endeavor to embrace: everything and everyone you love will die and be ripped away from you—that's the basis for the methodological elimination of desire and the cultivation of nonattachment. Notwithstanding the fact that I'd hurled my Buddhist texts against the walls, breaking their spines, the morning my father died, I found myself nearer to the path of acceptance of suffering than ever before. I had been forced deeper into her world, which was the only silver lining of my father's death.

Unfortunately for us both, we never figured out the detachment part. Her sorrow persisted and my bitterness swelled.

For example, Luke and I were to receive one Christmas card

that year, in contrast to the dozens that had covered my father's fridge in any prior December. It would seem that, with a sigh, maybe one last shiny tear, they all just crossed him—and us—out. We were to hear from less than six of those so-called friends of my father's after they walked out of the memorial we'd hosted for them that night, blurry with weeping, trembling with their release, like selfish lovers rolling away—spent.

As a rule, people suck, Serala might have warned me any number of times with a tight jaw. And this was the kind of thing that Jay and others meant when they said, *she's dark man, it's toxic.* But as the years piled up, so did the reasons to believe she spoke hard, unwelcome, but fundamental truths. And I preferred to see and speak plainly, especially then, when my father was irrecoverable and language was loathsome.

Eighteen

I MADE MY DRIVE ACROSS the top of America toward the East Coast and Serala in mid-August, Kaya panting in the shotgun seat. I had technically "broken up" with Mona but knew she was going to hang on in anyway she could. Devoid of the energy required to cauterize our split, I just went. In the trashy motels where I stopped, the story on the news was the blackout on the East Coast.

By the time I reach Serala, it's all over, electricity surging through wires as well as the bruised and stormy skies. Her hair is long and we both have new tattoos: hers are moons and stars, on her feet and covering scars. Mine is for my father, a sacred heart wrought with other tangled symbolism. We stand in her kitchen a bit awkwardly, just trying to figure out if we'll undress or not, drinking the end of a bottle of whisky. It's too hot to stay idle—I'm dripping even at nine o'clock—and we decide to start driving to visit Samar in Massachusetts.

It's far too late to bother Samar's family. Though it has been years since I was "with" her, her caustic mother and stepfather can still drive the fear in me. So we go walking through the serpentine streets of her wealthy town, heading for the beach, past places where she and I used to park her car and make it rock with passion under five fingered lightning and the crash of summer thunder.

After days in the truck, Kaya is tugging me left and right, desperate to be free of her leash. I'm catching Samar up on my mother's current conundrum: she has taken custody of twins we've known for years, one of them severely disabled, because their own mother is locked up and strung out.

I mean, she loves her kids, I say, referring to the jailed mom, *but she's a fucking junkie.*

The cicadas sing a few bars.

Sometimes you can be a real asshole, Serala announces, and crosses her arms and takes a couple of strides ahead of us. Samar decides it would be a good moment to lag behind. I can't find the words to apologize that night, probably because I didn't understand on an intellectual level what I'd done—only on an intuitive one. But I don't have to because Serala lets it go—with a kiss, or a laugh, or an arm looped through mine, we are soon reconciled.

We sit on a beach where Samar and I, as infantile leftists, once turned an American flag upside down early in the A.M. on the Fourth of July. Now the three of us drink twelve beers and watch Kaya and Knox crash back and forth, chasing nothing in the brackish surf, until day pushes the sky up with a rosy palm.

THE NEXT NIGHT WE WITNESS Samar perform in a cozy dive bar. The place is packed with regular boozers and we have to move along a wall to get close to the stage. In front of me, taking her pose beneath peach stage lights, Samar closes her eyes and begins. Behind me, Serala is managing to look tough enough that all of the boozehounds can only softball their hungry glances at her. I stay close, virtually at Samar's feet, and clap and whistle to compensate for the inattention she mostly receives. But I keep looking back at Serala and there the music glistens and widens her eyes, even makes her forget her cigarette growing ash in her hand.

She cops to the power Samar has after we hug Samar goodbye outside the lounge in the absolute black of a tenement shadow at midnight. As we hit the freeway, Serala says, *I feel like I want to hear Samar sing every song that I love* and we promise to make a mix tape in that spirit. We drive back to Brooklyn a little bit heavier, a little bit closer, too. For the first time in over a year, we make slippery love in one hundred percent humidity and then, in the morning, I drive back to Carolina.

AFTER MY FIRST GRADUATE YEAR exiled with Mona in a subdivision, I was finally moving into Wilmington proper: The ancient house on the edge of the vast ghetto loomed up, crooked with history. I was downtown—or right on the edge of the Historic District, depending on how you looked at it. The landlady called it a "transitional neighborhood," a real estate euphemism for black. The park across the street was carpeted with shattered bottles, drug baggies, and litter. Groups of idle men milled on the corners all day. It wasn't too wise to walk alone at night, but in the light of day it was a community, full of good and kind people who knew one another well.

Wilmington was full of ghosts, a fact fairly well accepted by the locals. I told Serala all this while she rocked in a chair on the porch on her first visit south, her cigarette dribbling blue. It had been a hundred and four years since the upstanding white citizens massacred the professional-class blacks in the only coup d'etat in U.S. history. Libraries and parks in other parts of town bore the names of the killers, but from my porch, behind the screen of Spanish moss, bougainvillea, and electrical wires, you could see the intersections and plots of land where the killing took place. Daily, I'm sure I waved to people who lost grandparents in that bloody string of days in 1898.

Roaches skittered over your toes on the sidewalks at night and the shadows were deep and rich. A freight train's blue horn rose from the north and the Cape Fear River carried in gusts from the sea. Wilmington was terribly, wonderfully haunted, and I think Serala loved that, I think that's part of why she came to visit twice in my first months of that year.

AT FIRST SHE WROTE THAT she felt safe there. She said, *Nothing for me is real or true till I say it to you.* She said it was enough: me, and bottles of wine, and sad music in that old Dixie city. But by her third letter, two-thirds through September and approaching the darkest part of the year, she was despairing again. *I'm really trying so hard this time, Eli. I know where this road goes,* she said, *I pray for a detour.* A presage of another winter, and her pain stole even more sleep. The moments she did manage to go under were again spoiled by nightmares she recounted in halting whispers on the phone while I tried to edit student essays and listen at the same time: people pulling out her perfect teeth, one by one, and she swallowed shards of enamel and mouthfuls of blood like almost drowning.

It feels like the pain is growing inside of me to take up all the space—leaving room for nothing else. Still sometimes I think maybe the pain is not growing but rather I'm shrinking around it. I wonder which is right—it could make all the difference.

For me, however, there were suddenly nights of music, soft light, and debauchery at the riverside. There was a tiny bar, which used to be a holding cellar for recently arrived slaves, where I drank in the horrid history and gin with manic poets. There was an antithetical sofa lounge on a second story where velvet chairs and couches held me as I slipped deeper into tipsy literary debate. I ran hard miles with Kaya through the Historic District and our adjoining ghetto almost every morning, wearing a groove into the town that made it feel known, something like home, even.

Meanwhile, I suddenly found myself as an adjunct professor—though they called us "TAs"—in charge of a section of Freshman Comp and Creative Nonfiction. I felt very little of the authority that I was entrusted with, and the nearly panicked fight to craft lesson plans and critique student papers exhausted but also thrilled me.

But messages Serala sent told me that as I eased closer to belonging, to faith in my own path, she was close as she'd ever been to the edge.

i wept for hours yesterday, maintaining a steady quiet kind of sob, at times building and pushing me from that gentle rocking into something like a storm. In moments, yesterday, i felt like the pain was pulling flesh and meat off bone, like my ribs were being stripped bare leaving everything stuck inside the cage open and unprotected. Then it would quiet itself.

In those rocking slower spaces yesterday, i thought of you. So much so, that at times i felt that i was not rocking, but it was you sitting behind me holding me. Waiting with me for the storms to come and pass. And all the words and screaming—the sounds of it all passed through me. It was like the rain down where you are, and how the clouds come.

Despite the tone, I was eager to convince myself that she was okay—a bit worse than normal, but okay—as if that were possible. Her letters stopped and her emails got short and her phone calls ended except for a few of that broken whisper.

. . . when sometimes i know i could—car into a wall or head in an oven, casually leave the gas on or even things less severe, just disappear for days. It takes every ounce of self control in me, every tool and trick i could use . . .

so . . . impulse control—don't take too many pills; don't do drugs; don't hurt yourself; don't go to people who hurt you; don't pack up and leave without telling anyone; don't scratch so much; don't hurt the people who love you for loving you; don't hurt other people because you're hurting; don't cry at work; don't let anyone see; don't say it out loud; don't just fucking don't.

Finally it was time to drive up and leave Kaya with her so I could fly home to a blue Christmas in my father's home.

The one night I spend with Serala that December, we take the dogs on a stroll to the little park near her Brooklyn apartment. The park is divided by some hedges and a cocky statue of Columbus placed there by "the Italian-American community with pride." It is snowing and the ground is already blanketed; our breath blurs the world. We're letting the dogs goof on the ice, holding onto one another for warmth. We begin to hear a man's shouts, punishing his dog viciously. The first couple eruptions elicit chuckles from us—who could get so worked up over a dog's mischief? When it continues unabated, though, our amusement dies. The tone of the man is sharpening with the dropping temperature. Finally we leash Knox and Kaya and walk around the hedges.

The man is framed against a chain-link fence; his dog cowers in front of him. He's showing it a tennis ball, then ramming the ball into the animal's snout and screaming, *You think this is a goddamn game? You stupid fucking animal, this is no goddamn game!* Then he chops the dog hard across the spine with the heel of his hand and that little snap in my gut that I've only felt a few other moments in my life happens. I'm walking toward him—and he's not a small guy. Serala backs me up, though, and as he sees us coming he hooks a rope on his dog, jerks it viciously, and begins walking toward the exit. He huffs past me, just hauling the dog, which Kaya snuffles at sympathetically. But Serala puts herself between him and the street, squares her shoulders, and shouts at him

You ought not have a dog if you don't like dogs, you fuck.

He pauses and I move closer to her. But after dueling her eyes for a moment, he puts his head down and gives her a wide berth as he leaves. He vanishes into the New York cold, pulling on that poor pooch's neck and cursing like muffled gunshots.

Still reckless and fearless and righteous, still living fully and standing up, even with a death wish swelling again in her breast.

IN THOSE PAST FEW MONTHS, without Serala in my life, I would have either blown my stack and done something wildly self-destructive or I would have done what many people watch themselves do when grief slaps them silly from out of nowhere: swallow it, move on, simply turn down the wick at one's center because life shouldn't be so well-illuminated anymore. But with her at my father's memorial, her prepping me with ferocious love before I faced Wilmington and all those people who would see me as *that haunted guy*, her with her way of teaching me that pain should lift your chin, brighten your eyes, make you say *fuck it*, that pain makes you wiser and stronger and you should embrace that—because of her I was not just tentatively able to return to the path that had been broken by the bubble racing to dad's lung, but I was able to return to it with determination, force, and pride. And so I looked up to her way of being and felt more bonded to her than ever.

So that night in Massachusetts when I spit the word "junkie" thoughtlessly, I wanted to tell Serala that I didn't think of her as a junkie, that she was so beautiful, and strong, and good that I couldn't. But I failed to see that she wore that badge not with shame—and not with pride—but with resignation. She felt solidarity with this faceless, nameless mother I was maligning. I'd negated the mother's love for her kids by that thoughtless sentence.

And I suspect I said "junkie" with the same vitriol one might say "nigger" or "raghead." My blindness reflected my elitism, and Serala, as a rule, rejected both.

Back in Carolina, I was becoming real to myself at last. The experiences that I was engaging were transforming the way I understood my theretofore youth. The delinquent hijinks and arrests, the drugs and betrayals, my father's life and death, the arduous journeys through other countries, all of the privilege I'd enjoyed—it was suddenly being translated into tangibility for the amorphous "reader." But also for myself. I felt wiser and stronger than I ever had, though also weary and still very deeply grieving my father, something I didn't share much except with her. I felt that because of the way Serala had helped me to weather death and see it through, the experience had improved me instead of ruined me; it had opened me instead of closed me, which is really the key, I still believe, to growth. What I failed to see then is that this was the very place where Serala and I split: as I rose with a new faith in myself fixed in place, ready to be weary forever, a little sad forever, but also strong forever, she came out the other side of loss just a little more tired each time. She'd long ago learned she could survive; it's just that she didn't want to.

Nineteen

MY EYES WERE ON THE calendar the rest of that semester. The moment I tied up the last loose end, I put Kaya in the shotgun seat, plugged in a Lucinda Williams tape, and drove off into the tranquil May sun of a war-frenzied America. I spent a northwest summer deep in a cocoon of marijuana, manual labor in the mountains, and the Novocaine nights of movies with Mona, praying for August. Serala wrote infrequently but intensely to me, relaying things that were as cyclical for her as the Mona roller coaster and aimless summer months were for me.

Over the last months I'd heard infrequent mention of this "boy," Jon, she was now kicking out of her life expressly because he had become more to her than a fling. There were dogs and music and curative laughter involved and she felt good with him. But in the heat of the summer he turned foolish and claimed he was in love. And so she stiff-armed him away.

The way that I found out was through one of her vague, sideways comments at the bottom of an email in the long summer of 2003:

It's hard. It's starting to hurt, i can't pretend. i feel it right now. It's almost over, i'll get his dogs tonight—give them away tomorrow and that will be all. Not a trace of him left, at least not in my life. But i'm a little bit scared.

He had called her and finally told her the truth about his anemia, the bored sockets of his eyes, the wincing pains, when the doctor told him the sarcoma would let him live just forty-eight more hours. He had called to say goodbye.

I know what she would say about the hurt. I can hear her saying it now: *It's mine, it's just for me.* Hoarding sorrow like a child hoards something sweet. But it wasn't sweet and the fallout demonstrated just how bitter, though the fallout surely had as much to do with not sleeping and slamming herself full of temporary numb as it did Jon's death.

Eli, there is a sound, i can't tell if it's ringing in my ears or my head. Horrible, i keep thinking of people screaming. The sound of women giving birth, violently. Like bodies burning, like children screaming and watching their own reflecting images in drops and pools of blood. In silence— all this pain—this sound that isn't real, only inside and i don't know where. It's quiet here, i know that. i'm not insane i know that too. Lately there has been this added thing. It's something deep, i thought it had to do with love, i thought it was about being alone. i think those things are wrong. But this sound that i hear, it's from the same place. An emptiness that echoes, a violence that's beyond terror. This is not a fear. It feels more real, like a truth, a loss. All the sounds of pain, vulgar and clear. A feeling like i know something horrible, i've seen something, lived it—but have no idea what. And i can count back the days, look at the notes and know where i've been. And nothing falls into this place. i know what i've been through, i've seen myself, my blood, my bruises, other hands—glass shattering. People dying. This is not the violence that i have lived through . . . and my shit, it's small—not so bad. This sound . . . i don't know what. It's shaking me, i'm shaking. i can't get to it, let alone explain . . . it's probably best left at this and not explained. Even if i could.

Before leaving Seattle for the long drive east, I tested Serala's waters, wanting to know what I was driving into—wanting to know, maybe, if I should skip New York this time around.

Let's go to the Jersey Shore, I said. *Let's rent a shitty room and write the shitty volume of poems like we always said we would. I'll bring the whisky and two pens.* The static on the line and the music behind her was all I heard at first. I anticipated the response.

I'm not going to have time for that, she said and I heard the thirsty drag off the cigarette. *Work is too much right now.*

Kaya bellied up to me, as if she understood the suggestion and would love to go to the shore. I rubbed her ears and waited to see if Serala would say more.

I better save all the patience I can for the next weeks, actually, she said, a theatrical weariness—versus the real weariness that I could recognize—under her words.

AFTER AN AMBIGUOUS SUMMER that left things even more muddled between us, I said goodbye to Mona in the forest fire-choked canyon of Missoula. She had landed a teaching fellowship in a women's studies program and so she had taken a deep breath and dove. She kissed me quick and hard, bit her lip and stepped to the curb. I watched her contrast there against the backdrop of a hunters' dive bar, dark skinned and so sad in that lily-white, sports-crazed town.

But she was on her road, and I was back to mine. We were technically still involved, but as far as I was concerned it was a technicality for the most part, part of a molasses-slow process of separation. I coughed through the hazy west, helicopters dangling totes of water the size of small cars into the crackling forests. The interstates were heavy with heat, Kaya panting more and more as we crossed into the damp east.

When I whip around a bustling Brooklyn corner and find Serala waiting for me at the entrance to her new apartment building, I can see the twenty-five-year-old business ace, forged. Not even a shred remained of the punk-rock artist aesthetic that had been her cocoon when I met her seven years earlier. Stilettos and leather briefcase, many ounces of silver jewelry sliding on wrists and chest as she paces—struts, really—with oblivion to everything around her. She waves to greet me—and to postpone our greeting, because she is yelling into her phone. I clamber out with odds and ends under my arms, a very emotional Kaya leashed to my wrist. I can hear Serala over the grinding of traffic and beats of calypso music floating by and the discussions fired in Puerto Rican Spanish.

No—no! Goddamn it, Donald, now you're just wasting my time. I asked you for all of those files on Friday—this is Tuesday, Donald. Do *you think I have time for this shit?* She pauses for a drag of her smoke and lets Donald squirm on the other end of the line while she pulls off her shades and rolls her eyes. *I hope you can handle it. I hope you handle it* now.

She flips her phone closed and, with her perfect smile, endures Kaya's gregarious hello.

My version of New York had changed: Luke had arrived in the city to finally finish his college career at NYU and Serala had moved into a luxury apartment, high on a Brooklyn hill. At first I couldn't comprehend the square footage, the balcony right out at the feet of the city, helicopters buzzing around it in the humid shimmer, like yellow jackets on a flower. I chose to see it as a sign that she was doing better.

The doorman nods at me as Serala and I struggle through the door with bags and the hyper dog.

Must be your brother that's already up there, he says and grins.

I can't say exactly when Luke and Serala started to become close. But by this time they are—hanging out far more than I am with either one of them. While some of it is small-hour cocaine mania, they also idle Sunday afternoons, chatting and watching films. He's had her presence at his back as he's thrashed through the grief for our father and then the disorienting move to New York. Not to mention that Luke has contended almost exclusively with immature females in his short life. Serala is a grand departure and just maybe the older sister he didn't get.

The door to her apartment is cracked; laughter and smoke somersault into the hallway. I unleash Kaya, who leaps with her whimpering cries of joy into the space. I hear Luke exclaim her name and I step in to see him pinned on the sofa beneath Kaya's hefty paws, half-heartedly dodging licks, holding his spliff high, smiling and laughing, Knox nosing in jealously.

How's the Rotten Apple, kids? I ask and Luke and his girlfriend Adaline go on about school, about the apartment they've found on the edge of Spanish Harlem. When I've done the requisite petting of Knox, Serala comes to me with a glass of wine and a kiss. The city's silhouette blazes through the window.

Let's paint the town, fuckers, she says at the end of a Pixies disc.

In pairs we negotiate the throngs, close together, walking fast on New York streets. We settle into a booth at a place called Silver's. It's full of tattoos, Elvis Costello glasses, wide-gauge piercings, absurdly loud indie rock, and screamed conversations. We all lean in—away from the hipsters, Luke and I on one side of the table, Serala and Adaline pressed close on a bench seat across—yelling at each other over beer and whisky. Luke gets up for a piss and I watch Serala speaking in Adaline's ear. Adaline's slender arm cocks her cigarette away as she brushes her auburn hair back and leans in close. Her green eyes spin, processing whatever my best friend is sharing with her—it looks important from here. As another tune breaks and whines out of the jukebox and the room swims through banks of clove smoke, Serala laughs with her, lights her Camel, puts a hand on her shoulder, and that is it. Adaline's in with me.

I don't recall much of those few days, actually, between the heat and the napping and the booze, but I know that Serala and I slept together tenderly then, arms twined or my head pressed to her breast, in the middle of that stifling month. She kept the window open and long, white drapes billowed over us.

An email that chased me back down the coast was sweet and buoying with the promise of a better year.

i'm glad that you came . . . i'm thankful for what i've got and i'm not worried anymore . . . i think you did a good job without me. i see a difference, a new kind of patience in you . . . before, for all these years, i was sure of my love for you. And now i'm sure that i love you, for who you are. For who you've always been to me, past the time and gaps and change . . . i'm not scared anymore, of time in between. i only miss you in between.

BACK DOWN IN WILMINGTON I faced a heavier teaching load and the daunting task of assembling a book-length thesis by April. But I found myself pleased to be back in the city. There was a nook of a room hung on the backside of our ancient house. I moved my desk out of my bedroom and against a peeling wall, beneath abundant light, amid husks of roaches and yellow jackets. Through the dirty panes I could see the center of our block's backyards, Carolina's nature rioting with ivy, Spanish moss, bougainvillea, feral cats and families of squirrels. Kaya could spend hours on the back porch, watching the creatures dart with a Zen intensity. My writing came easier with the change of venue and the nascent manuscript thickened. My roommate, Smith, brewed cherry and muscadine wine and we grew close over long idle nights, rocking on the front porch and sensing the lightless ghetto below, sharing our favorite albums.

But by the time that October ended, Serala was nasty, sometimes mean. It was that time of year again: wet and dark but also the beginning of a lineup of hard anniversaries, beginning with her birthday, which she could scarcely tolerate. She fought with me tooth and nail over stupid things late nights on the phone.

I'm standing in the kitchen, spinning a glass of muscadine on our sticky counter, looking out at the big oaks, alive with busy families of feral cats. Kaya's got her paws on the sill, interested but thwarted by the barrier of glass. The cordless phone against my head is getting uncomfortable, just as the conversation has.

So . . . the rejection letters keep rolling in, but I keep sending essays out. Got a professor who says to keep them all and wallpaper your bathroom someday—God knows I'll have enough.

Serala makes a sound of disgust, blows a drag of smoke out hurriedly.

God, that's fucking asinine. Throw them away, Eli. Why would you hold onto rejection?

Her tone is out of all proportion to the topic. I try not to match it. I swallow some wine, turn away from the window.

Well, I mean I guess his point is that one day they will be laughable. Or maybe he thinks it's valuable to remember how hard you've had to try.

Yeah, well, he's an idiot. Who needs a reminder of how hard they have to try? Who isn't aware of it every fucking day?

I say I suppose that's true, kill the muscadine, beg off the phone—till the next round.

But I knew that she had to tighten up her shell, wax her shield, draw down her masks; I knew the process. In other conversations when she began to break and weep, her turmoil was clearer. But all this fury, I knew, was better—if things became truly as bad as they could be, I wouldn't hear a whisper.

THE FIRST RUMORS OF JACK may have come in an email I've lost, or it may be that Serala found the voice to tell me in person. I know that by the time she sailed down the coast in December for a visit, she was well down the road with Jack. She'd known him since she was a teenager but until then nothing had ever blossomed between them besides drug-addled hijinks and platonic affection. I remember it as funny—chuckling at her as she tried to explain it.

I don't know. I've known him for so long and I don't think there was ever anything there. She sits in a rocker on my porch, smoking. *I guess just because he was far away, because he had that brat, I never looked at it as possible.* Across the street in the park, the blanket of shattered bottles divvies up the moonlight, and she fixes it with a stare and I know not to chuckle more. This is serious—a real conundrum.

And I knew she was serious when she stopped calling his son *brat*. She never stopped referring to children in general that way, but Raymond became his *kid,* or his *son,* or *Raymond.*

That December weekend we hauled Knox and Kaya down to the empty, gusty beaches where Knox sprinted for miles after birds. She ran until she was as small as the gulls in our sight, then ripped all the way back like someone had just then plugged her into her racing dog genes. Kaya tried to keep up but she was oafish and lumbering in comparison, and so she took to trying to chase her down, nip her heels, make Knox stop outshining her.

We walked miles in the woods, the tropical forest finally giving up the green ghost in the face of winter. We ate venison tenderloin that Smith himself had shot some days before. It was wrapped in bacon, and we drank his muscadine like beer. I thought his and Serala's mutual passion for rare meat and hard wine might just carry them off to elope right then—me, Jack, and the rest of the world be damned. We went and saw the dumb Will Ferrell film *Elf*, and she laughed and laughed, and put her arm in mine afterwards in the glow of the marquee. And we stayed in bed (innocently) a lot, just slugging wine and talking away. She tossed it off, but I know it was true: she was a little happy. She had told me less than a year ago that being in love was probably all done for her.

> *i don't know if it's possible for someone to get so close. It seems like some places are just hard and closed for good. And even if i did, who could know me so well and still be able to love me like that? And why would anyone want to? i have nice tits, but they're not that nice.*

They referred to Jack's father as "The Doctor" because he had survived a full career as a junkie; he got two of his three sons high for the first time, too. After I met the man, I had a face to go with the image of a father's hand smacking forearm flesh on his young son, raising a vein to bring him the greatest pleasure imaginable. The Doctor was a pale shell by the time I encountered him, dying fast of cancer, but unflappable as far as I could tell with his medical marijuana and stashes of pills. I wanted to know the nature of this thing Serala was in, the family she was necessarily imbibing to love Jack. After her initial guarded enthusiasm came a chapter when she stepped back and wanted to pretend like it was just drugs.

We just fucking get high together; it's just safer that way, it doesn't mean anything.

But he started to move his things down to Brooklyn from Boston where he'd been a carpenter for years. Ostensibly it was to be with his father but he began spending most nights with Serala. She rode the swells of junkiedom with him and that should perhaps have made me hate him. Sure, they enabled one another, but I know that at least sometimes they kept each other strong, that the sex and the tenderness and the booze were enough. But from where I was standing it didn't much matter; she'd never stayed clean for too long and I was a hell of a lot less worried about her scoring smack with a big, strapping cat like Jack than her slinking down to the ghettos in her fancy car alone. Or, worse, going to see someone she used to know.

I started to hear different things—going up to Boston just for fun, camping plans, even in the winter, learning to fish—and a different tone. A silent reversal started to take place in me then: I allowed optimism to slide back into my heart. *Just maybe,* I thought, *just maybe this will fucking do it.*

THE THING THAT STRUCK ME the first time I saw him—on a weekend jaunt north—was that he looked, to me, very much like Hugh. He was big, and tough, and restive in the shotgun seat next to me. We were feeling each other out. We ate sunflower seeds and said manly things about fishing and trucks—two subjects I know very little about. But by the time we were ensconced in soft light and hard drink, I felt easy. I decided to be happy for Serala.

We're in her spare bedroom and the hour is small; she's yanked the sheets away from me, scoffing at my sloppy, male approach to the project. She's tucking in a corner when he wanders in and sits down on the floor next to me.

You know, you could change the sheets on your bed, too, he says, looking up at her. I don't remember what she says exactly, but it is something along the lines of *why don't you go do it your fucking self. Well, it's just that this is your home and I'm a guest here. The way I look at things it's a matter of hospitality—we're not in my home.*

It might have been a tense and nasty moment if I hadn't watched his eyes dancing and her faux-fist attack, which he rendered futile with a big laugh, tying her skinny arms in knots.

And:

We're at his family's narrow, manufactured home, Serala paying her respects to his father, me just trying to stay out of the way. There is a big-screen TV and a length of very soft couch; his father is counting out pills on the coffee table with skeletal fingers. The cop show on the screen is turned up a bit loud for conversation. Jack is fidgety in his seat and I don't know if he's feeling pressure to facilitate conversation, is worried over his dad's present state, or just needs some kind of fix. Serala slips out for a cigarette, leaving me in the lap of a sad and edgy scene.

Pop, hey, you want to trade some of that oxycodone for some high-grade pot? I've got about an eighth of it.

Jack is hunched over his knees, rocking his bulky frame and twisting hands, muscles shaping in his forearms, looking eagerly toward his father now. A grin is parked, out of kilter, on his face, awaiting an answer—but really awaiting a slice of attention, approval. I can hear it all so clearly somehow, everything I feel I could learn about the situation: a hard-living, but good-hearted man, appealing to his father for approval, for engagement, for something resembling validation. Appealing to the person whose expression of love has been exactly this: the sharing of drugs. All the reciprocal love is in the timbre of Jack's voice, in the anticipatory way his green eyes are trained on his father's sallow, expressionless profile. Serala slips back in as quietly as she slipped out. The open door shoves a brief wedge of brightness across the room and Jack's father squints and blocks his eyes. Then, as shadow re-consumes us, he grunts and shrugs his agreement to Jack, who lights up momentarily, and I realize that he never had any more of a chance than his father now does. And I realize that my father *did* have a chance—and he took it. The chord of that vibrates enough bittersweet light through me to get out of that trailer dry-eyed and whole.

And:

We're sitting at brunch at the Montrose Café: Serala, me, Luke, and Jack. It's a fancy affair, the brunch menu: eggs Benedict, Florentine, Belgian waffles and croissant French toast, mimosas. Serala is staring down her bloody Mary, stirring; Luke is preparing his Irish coffee; I'm being good and drinking iced tea. Jack is wearing a button-down shirt and has shaved. He's ordered a single whisky for the morning, but when they bring it in a shot glass he says:

Bring me a tumbler, will ya?

Not rude, but enough edge in the tone to say that they should have known.

It's just that I wanted a neat drink is all, Jack says, sounding kind of bored, *I mean, it's just the beginning of the day.*

He takes two Valium from his breast pocket and throws them back with his ice water. It strikes me then that this is serious business for him—he even looks the part of the casual businessman: getting fucked up. *This is how you start. This is what you do on Sunday while your father lies dying.*

One Tuesday in mid-May, university duties at last complete, I am sitting in my dusty nook, dueling my completed thesis manuscript that nevertheless still needs major surgery before it goes out into the hands of the agents and editors of the world. Kaya is stalking a nattering squirrel at the bottom of the stairs. Carolina blue skies and the explosion of spring. Mona calls. I groan inwardly, expecting another exhortation to get my ass on the road to her bungalow in Montana, though my rent is paid through May and Wilmington has turned sweet enough for me to want to stay a while.

Hey, baby, I say.

Hey, Mona says, and I can hear her smoking, which means she has something to say. Outside, Kaya commits to action and hurtles down the stairs with a series of thumps; the squirrel skedaddles, and she yips once in frustration.

So, I met this boy today.

It's funny how fast and distinctive jealousy is—a plunge of ice water through my veins. I gather myself and play it as cool as I can. This is a great deal more effortful than I'd thought it would be—I'd been telling myself for months, if not years, that I wished Mona would meet someone else.

Okay. Well, what does that mean exactly?

I don't know. A maddeningly long silence while she smokes. *I guess maybe I want to go out with him.*

Okay . . .

What was there to say to that? She exhaled brashly and then sighed.

I don't know, Eli. I just feel like I've not really established my own life here—I've been hiding out all the time. And now everything is blooming, and people are coming out of their houses, and I have some real friends . . .

It's cool, Mona, I say through gritted teeth, *you can have whatever you need. Do your thing. I'd like to stay here a while anyway.*

I was pissed, and I was hurt, and I decided I couldn't sit in Wilmington any longer mourning the end of my days there. So I left Kaya with Smith, drove to Raleigh, and got a plane to go to Serala quick, to my consolation. Her, as a place—the only one I could go to with my quiet hurt.

I DON'T KNOW WHERE JACK is. It's just Serala and me that night. I've gotten in late, even by her standards. I deliver the news of Mona over our second bottle of wine. She just shakes her head.

Mona's a fucking moron, she says, and there is more bite behind her words than mere ego mending. *I know you love her, Eli, and I know you've thrown a lot of years into this. But neither one of those are good enough reasons to keep this shit up.*

Soon my head swims, partly from the wine, partly because my mind does not want to consider the level of cowardice I possess with respect to Mona. So we crawl into bed, beneath that flapping white curtain, in that sweet bed that has held me so many years with its heavy blankets. When I put my hand under her neck and pull her beneath me I do not feel any hesitation and we tangle up like always in the candle's dance. But very soon she goes still. She puts her hand on my chest.

I can't do this, she says. *No, I can't.*

She is apologetic, and mixed up, and almost changes her mind, but I am far away by that point. I feel like the most lecherous fuck on the planet, to say nothing of a bad friend—to both her and Jack. Any doubts about this thing between them are smoke.

But I sleep like a tired dog with my head on her breast and the springtime breathing through the room.

In the morning I am closed into her room and in the living room I hear a strand of angry words. Jack is back and I get very worried. Not so much that Jack is going to hand me my ass, but more that I will be the thing that fucks this up for Serala.

She and Jack continue the fight outside on the sidewalk. It is a strangely cool and bleary May day, but both of them have their opaque shades on, their tense gestures bouncing off each other, like street theater. I drag Knox and Kaya toward a scrap of grass, and the way Jack is tongue-lashing Serala, and the way she is listening to him, I think the worst. So when she tells me it was all over something else, something obscure, something that *doesn't fucking matter anyway*, the cool hand of relief runs down my spine.

We drop Jack off at the tiny house he shares with his struggling family. He and I hug each other goodbye; one of us makes a suggestion about him coming out to Seattle with her in August, maybe bringing Raymond, too, to see the Northwest. I climb in Serala's blue car for one last ride to North Carolina and watch Jack fade away in the rearview, pale against the pale house.

WHEN SERALA DITCHED PALLIATIVE possibilities I always got anxious. That's why I tried to get her into a bungalow on the Jersey Shore, force her to punch out the poetry that it seemed to me had kept her alive like breath back in college, but she wanted me to believe she was done with art. Moreover, she wanted to believe it herself. The hazards of being open enough for poetry were too great—that was the point of her climb into the corporate saddle: to close certain doors inside. Serala was such a searingly honest person that I didn't understand she sometimes had to deceive herself. I'd read her emails and letters and lament the loss of her voice from the world of poetry. I was slow on the uptake, as fooled by her as she was by herself.

the way that things look different in the light
even when it's just the clouds reflecting
like dull steel
and today i can't tell which one was lying
how things in the dark hold softness or
if it's only the shadows of the things themselves
that are soft
but this morning
i prayed
for the light not to break
so hard, and for warmth
and then for strength

and when i got in the shower and wept,
i waited for the warmth to wash over inside
i rinsed my hair and thought of you.

Last night i sat out on the balcony in the rain
and watched a storm rage and the river thrash in
solidarity. There was no distinction that i could
make between the lightning and city lights. It
was not a storm raging over the city; the city was
the storm. And in that sliver of an hour, early in

the a.m., i watched time turn over on itself, i sat
there soaked and waiting for the pale blue light to
come. Shivering, i wished for you.

Her art was alive and well; creation was bearable in disguise.

Likewise, anything resembling traditional love was off-limits, or so she'd have both of us believe. And I did until Jack materialized. It was appropriate that he was an old figure, a time-faded if handsome kid that I remembered from photos before my time in her life. The impression that Monty had left on me was that he was her last attempt to fit into any traditional container of relationship and that when that failed (and it failed early on), she just dialed her love for him into a different frequency and simultaneously allowed me closer, compensating for the lack of a life partner with the presence of a highly unorthodox best friend.

The momentum with Jack was strange, huge but not yet fast, like the first rotation of a boulder at the top of a slope. She spooked, of course, and tried to downplay it, but I was almost giddy with her failure to do so. When Mona decided to take another man for a spin and I ran to Serala's bed, I was caring for my ego, sure, but I was also testing Serala—both motivations unconscious at the time; I was merely doing what was normal between us by then. When she turned me down, my shame and moderately injured pride were nothing compared to the conviction that came down with her hand on my chest that May night: what she had found was real.

Of course it was also a liability because Jack was less scrupulous than even she was about the substances he used to push the long sadness of his life out of his veins, mainly because he'd been instructed and even encouraged to do so since he was small. But there comes a juncture in every treatment when risky methods are called for and, from where I was standing, it seemed as if Jack vanquished Serala's symptoms in a few short months of feverish— if junkie—love.

Twenty

LEAVING WILMINGTON DAMN NEAR broke my heart, as I belatedly realized I'd come to love the city almost like a person—and to love several people who would remain there. I drove south slowly, trying to soul-search but really just delaying the inevitable arrival at Mona's door. Between Florida and Montana, I made up and changed my mind a dozen times about going to her. She was begging at this point, terrified that her fling was going to cost her my love.

Between Houston and Grand Junction, Colorado, Mona leaves me forty-three voice mails in one day. That should have been clue enough about the nature of this relationship, but at the time it just felt like more evidence that I didn't have a choice. When I arrive, trying to keep the equilibrium I've cultivated on the highways, I find I can't. As the June Montana sun is cut by the Venetians and the dogs worry at the foot of the bed, stirring up cyclones of dust motes, I swallow half a bottle of wine and let the demons out.

If you really think that you can put me on hold, fuck someone else, and then bid me to come back, you're fuckin' tripping, Mona, I manage to say before I fall to tears—more at my cowardly inability to walk away than anything else.

But we had it out with enough fury and then enough tenderness to make me believe we'd turned a corner—after four years of roller coaster straight-aways. I allowed myself to settle back into us, reapplying myself to the exhausting task of *making it work.* As if it we were a problematic but possibly timeless novel. After failing to leave Mona as many times as I had, a belief had wired into my brain: I couldn't do it. It was absolutely suffocating to think of never getting free of her, so I told myself the palliative, cowardly lie that eventually *she'd* be the one to end it.

There was no Sprint coverage in Missoula so my cell didn't even have a chance to ring the next day.

I was sleeping hard, my head packed beneath two pillows. Then I walked the bucolic neighborhoods of Missoula sipping coffee, feeling out the place I was to call home in the autumn. Serala left me two messages that morning. She was fucked up in a way that I'd never heard: desperate, quiet sobs, scared, not stoic at all then. *Jack's had kidney failure,* she said, *he's really bad.*

When I called I got his brother, because Serala was in with Jack. I told him I'd pray, instinctively, as if I had a rosary on hand. He said he'd like that, and so I did my best with my breathing and my silence.

When she called back the next day he was brain-dead. That's what she said, her voice breaking, loud and then a whisper over just those few syllables: *Jack is brain-dead.* They were going to do some more tests to make sure, but if the results came back as expected, they'd pull the plug in the morning. With Jack in that state Serala had time to talk—before she split with Jack's brothers and best friend, Thomas, to erase all hope, to start the bitter celebration. She spoke in a flat monotone mostly, but with weepy breaks, too. The story was:

They go camping—in any other context this would make me laugh. I like to picture it. They drive deep into some Connecticut forest and start hiking. Jack seems as if under a spell out there, full of pep and chatter, and Serala finds herself able to follow, a six-pack and a bottle in her hands, for hours and hours. They find their spot, the perfect spot, and make it home for the night (I imagine her making beds in the tent, folding over the corners of the sleeping bags for easy access). They talk, and drink, and laugh, and there are no pills, no junk, nothing, aside from maybe a skinny joint or two and that booze. They make love and Serala sleeps, for hours, and they descend the next day as euphoric as they climbed and, in some kind of celebration, kill the first of two bottles of Maker's Mark by the time they roll back into Boston. They go out for sushi— counterbalancing, I suppose, the grittiness of nature—and drink sake, and laugh, and it's then that he tells her: it has been the best night of his life.

But then they are bound for the hospital to visit Jack's rapidly dying father, where Jack accepts a crack rock from his youngest brother instead of money he is owed. Jack and Serala smoke it together, a searing, bright burn right through the filmstrip of the day, erasing all that might have been right. Back at her place they find that the cycle has begun, and they score and start shooting. When he begins to complain about back pain, Serala tries to rub it out, assuming the strain of a long hike has shifted a disc or pulled a muscle. But when he exclaims, suddenly, waking from a nod, *When the fuck is the ambulance coming?* she calls one and starts flushing whatever junk is left. In the ambulance he is lucid and quiet, clutching her hand, I imagine. In the hospital, he seems all right and is even working on one of those *New York Times* crosswords with her; some of the sweetness from the best night reenters his face. But the toxicology screen is taking a while and Serala steps from the room to go walk Knox, and the pain gets worse, and he screams, and so they shoot him with Demerol, and he falls into respiratory arrest.

If she had been right there, she wouldn't have let them do it, but she was away, momentarily, believing by then that he'd be fine and she didn't have to tell them about the junk. She couldn't imagine that this night, in an ER with doctors everywhere, he would go. She'd told me of the several nights when Jack shot too much and she found herself kneeling over him on the hardwood floor, rescue breathing—breathing for him—as she'd learned as an EMT on the interstates years before. She said it was too ironic— these were the only moments when she felt almost incapable of staying awake: when his life had depended on it. As if sleep were a siren song. But she always had saved him.

THAT DAY, MONA AND I stroll by the Clark Fork River with Kaya, and her dog, Kasko, and Louis's dog, Sasha, which Mona has kidnapped with the promise of a better life in Missoula than Seattle. I'm learning that the Montana skies are as big as they say. I am looking at them and they're almost pure blue, tiny braids of cloud here and there, like strands of hair floating on the breeze. I feel sort of consoled by how puny we are. The river is flowing with gusto, up to the brim with snowmelt, and people are sparse along the banks because school has been out a few days already. Kaya is happy to be back with her pack. Mona and I are holding hands, and I wonder if the relative peace I can access here, now, while Serala is hurting so fucking bad, is wrong.

And then Sasha struggles up the steep, overgrown bank of the river. In her square jaws, she is clutching a spinal column twice her own length. A slick membrane of skin still sheaves half of it. I cannot begin to guess at why this sends me reeling into an almost nauseous panic.

Later that day we are up in the canyon above the town, getting the dogs good and tuckered out before I catch a flight to Serala's side. Sasha is lagging behind, sniffing at the breeze quizzically, despite my hollering. I look back after a moment and she is rolling like dogs do to cover themselves in the canine perfumes of shit and rot. I dash back, give her a little kick, and she jumps up—revealing an entire leg of a deer. The hoof is still attached and all the fur intact; the top of the leg is raw and bloody, as if someone has just ripped it off a passing doe. The way this frightens and baffles me is out of proportion to reason. Surely there is an explanation for these gruesome finds—hunters, or bobcats, or something. But that wouldn't soothe me; I know with certainty that Sasha leads me to these things for a reason. Maybe she is showing me—and dogs, after all, are capable of such things—what is happening inside of Serala: violence, rending apart.

WHEN I LAND AT JFK, I see her first. She is all blurry with whisky and old tears. The carousel is churning bags out and she watches it like it's a movie. Knox is leashed to her wrist, doing those nervous little high steps around her, just like the day we broke her out of the pound in San Diego. When I hug Serala I can feel all the bones, feel the broken sips of air she takes, like each breath is partly sob. But her eyes are dry, just bruised and puffed, and she is paler than I've ever seen. She looks like shit. I don't speak until we get to the car and, because I want to clear it out of my throat before the wild driving, I say:

God, I'm so fucking sorry, love.

I think I can get it out and stay tough, be a rock for her to cling to right from go, but it breaks halfway out of my mouth. I swallow and hold onto her neck for a while. She points out the Jack Daniel's on the floorboard, twists the volume knob, lights a smoke, and wheels out to the road.

At the entrance to the turnpike she files into the cash lane accidentally and then swings right into the E–Z Pass line, nosing in front of a white Cadillac that is still a few feet back. But the driver doesn't like it and he rolls forward, making a point of keeping his head out the window as his car passes, just centimeters from our fender.

You better watch where the fuck you coming from, he says, in the nasal tones of an old Jersey Italian.

I look at Serala and she has a steady wildness in her eyes, a rage I haven't seen before. He is still hanging his head out, alternating his gaze from the inch between the two fenders to her face, challenging her, and I suddenly know she is going to mash the pedal and cave in his door. I put a hand on her arm and lean out the window and tell him there's *no problem,* tell him to *be cool,* and he is. And Serala starts breathing again, and thanks me, and reaches for the bottle instead.

Her place is packed with Boston kids, coworkers and Jack's surrogate little brothers. They sound exceedingly young to me, and I realize Serala scarcely knows them. Three blunts are circling around, and there is a bottle within reach wherever you stand or sit. Lucinda Williams is doing her cool blue wailing on the box, and there is the skyline, bright like a fistful of stars has been hurled at the city, and so I shake hands, nod, and accept a joint and open a beer like I'm arriving at a party, and I guess I am. And Jack's best friend comes through the door.

The last time I'd seen Thomas was eight years back, when he was a dreadlocked traveling kid, killing springtime at the parties of Sage Hill. Serala has kept me posted over the years on his travels, his fights with drugs and the law. And she's made sure that I know how much he means to her and how hard he's tried, all cleaned up, to get her and Jack to do the same. Thomas is a hell of a lot bigger than I recall. His hair is short and his arms are thick. A fresh tattoo of an angel stands raised on one forearm. He has the half-cracked look of drunken grief, and he hugs me hard, like a brother, me almost disappearing in his arms. I realize in that moment that although I don't have any claim to a friendship with Thomas, except by proxy, that he sees an ally in me—someone else who works at the task of keeping her above ground. He thanks me and thanks me for coming, and I am reminded of just how well Serala represents me in my absence. I try to think of what to say, but I can't imagine what words could mean to someone who just lost their best friend.

AROUND EVERY CORNER, BEHIND EVERY bottle of wine, through the thick smoke of blunts and Pall Malls, a tripwire of grief might be stretched. But there are other moments, too, other surprises—even some fun. I remember rolling out to the Jersey Shore in the massive truck that Thomas' girl has rented to drive us around in. The windows are down, cigarettes fired, Serala's hair snapping like it always has on the freeways, Springsteen on the box and up fucking loud. We've finally made it to the Jersey Shore after many plans had imploded over the years. She and I slip away to walk Knox on the boardwalk, against the fierce wind that seems to blow so hard from the north that it still carries a bite of spring. She shivers in her loose skin.

Samar arrives one day to comfort us with her songs, her steady presence, her courage in the face of pain. I remember her and Serala disappearing into the bedroom. Serala just stands up, as if instinct calls, takes Samar's hand, and walks away, the bedroom door clicking shut gently. I hope that they won't come out until morning, maybe that embrace will be enough to carry Serala to sleep. They can exchange their toughness for the reverse, for the tenderness that rules them both on the safe side of walls. But soon Serala emerges to kneel by the stereo, playing one sad song after another: PJ Harvey, Nick Drake, Jeff Buckley, Elliott Smith, Lucinda, the Pretenders, Alison Krauss, Neil Young. I wake at the crack of a pink dawn to walk Samar to the ferry, then find Thomas in bed with a Budweiser, staring at the molding that he and Jack put up along the ceiling a week earlier. One shiny tear stands on his cheekbone.

And through all of it, Serala mostly refuses words. The one sentence I recall vividly comes as I am leaving. The street is washed in New York's extreme June sun; the rays are splintering off every piece of glass and metal like pinwheels scattered. She holds me tightly, her face against my chest as the Cuban driver leans on his town car, looks at his watch pointedly, and sighs. I am dredging myself for something right to say, something loving that will not come off as simple pressure to *keep on keepin' on*. She lifts her face and puts me at arm's length. Then she looks me in the eye and says it: *The whole time I was with him, I never thought about dying.*

I FLEW HOME TO SEATTLE for the summer. I was semi-diligent about calling Serala, but she wasn't often up for talking much. She was still just boycotting language. And I knew she was busy with work and, more, with Jack's family.

In the meantime she wrote me emails with titles like "New York is flooding, slowly, as I type." She never said much except for things about the sky or what Thomas was up to. But it was enough to allow me to keep tabs; she didn't want me to worry more. And finally she told me she was coming to visit.

> *i guess i bought a plane ticket sometime on Saturday. i don't remember doing it, i don't remember anything about the last two days other than swinging my head back to a bottle and swallowing hard to get pills down. Just that, over and over again.*
>
> *There's something to be said for repetition.*

Even though only two and a half months had passed since Jack's funeral, I wasn't prepared for how furiously she was still grieving in August. I expected her to be able to do it like she always had: suck it up and stomp forward and pretend. Not that I wanted for her to do that with me. But when she entered the house crowded with me, Mona, Luke, and Adaline, and dogs, I could see the fault lines and fractures; I knew when Serala went to the bathroom if she was peeing or getting high; I watched her step out to the porch and face the skyline to weep beneath sunglasses.

We spent a quiet and restorative couple of days in the mountains with my mother, watching eagles cut the sky and horses gallop on the meadow's edge. Everyone but Serala spent hours in the cold green water of the Wenatchee River, washing the dust of mountain life away. She didn't even sweat.

The second night there I am scrubbing pots and daydreaming. The sun is making an ornate exit and a breeze is coming up, shivering the pines and combing out the willow tree. As I move to put away a bowl, I gain the view from another window and see that Serala and my mother are sitting side by side on the sagging steps of the deck. The wind is making Serala's hair wild and stealing the ash from her cigarette and my mother is looking at her. I know it with an instinctive gut punch: they are talking about Jack—and, just maybe, people my mother has lost. It might be the first real conversation they have ever had. Serala swigs on a beer and nods and I turn back to the sink, feeling like I've intruded.

So the visit is not a cure, of course, scarcely a Band-Aid maybe, but she isn't doing worse. Her last night arrives and we haven't yet been out for a fine meal, so Luke and I search for clean shirts, Mona and Adaline spend an hour in the bathroom, and Serala waits, already dressed, killing the last of the house's wine.

We find a fancy steak and seafood house on Elliott Bay, the rolling spill of Seattle lights on all sides of us out on the patio. The night starts off well enough with the first couple of bottles:

run-of-the-mill talk about food, wine, war, a toast to Jack, et cetera. But then the rain starts, and we move inside the restaurant, and Serala's eyes go darker, and she starts drinking faster and mistreating the waitress, and I know this is not a happy road. And she cuts loose, grief and a nice cabernet stomping all over the nice dinner.

You guys have it all so wrong, she slurs, referring now to the question of "drama" in a relationship. *If you knew for just a minute what it was like to lose your lover you would feel stupid and small for all the bullshit.*

And there I am, urging her on in my head. I want Mona to hear what she has to say. I think Mona might listen, but I am overestimating her willingness to hear Serala in this state. Serala lurches further along the monologue, spilling wine. Other diners slide looks at us, and Mona and Adaline blush and turn away from her.

I might fuck somebody for drugs but so what? I might fuck Jack's brother now because he looks like him, so the fuck what? It's too fucking hard. All there is, all there is, is pain and seconds of escape. And you can't reject anything that brings you a little bit of sweet. Stop wasting fucking love.

A gulp and a deep drag are her punctuation and it is time to go.

At home the chasm yawns wider between me, Serala, Luke, and the two girlfriends. We light candles on my father's shrine and weep; we throw more wine back recklessly. We kneel and talk to my father; we inhabit the chaos of grief, clutching at the opportunity to yank some of it out of our chests. With Serala at my side, I let myself into the space that I ordinarily can avoid: rage. As the flames dance in front of photos, I catch isolated glances from my father on the glossy surfaces. I let myself feel it, then let myself say it, make it as real and present as I can: *He wanted to live so badly, finally, and he was cut down right at the fucking beginning.* Serala makes for the bathroom to get high—again. Resentful and restive, I think about marching to the bathroom and demanding a shot of the relief she has—to point out to her that I don't have any relief. Instead, I march into the bedroom where Adaline and Mona are sort of angrily cowering and pull the .45 from the bedside table.

What the fuck are you doing? Mona demands, and perhaps it is a very ugly tone or, perhaps not—maybe I just want war.

I'm putting the fucking gun on his fucking shrine, I spit. *The gun that he just barely didn't use to kill himself.*

I treat Mona and Adaline irrationally, poorly. As if by way of not yet knowing the flooring, defacing power of grief, they have betrayed us.

In the morning I stumble up in time to take Serala to the airport. We hold hands in the rich sunlight spiking off the carapaces of jumbo jets. We promise we'll see each other soon—but we do not have a plan.

Twenty-One

MONA'S SEMESTER STARTED AND I settled in earnestly in Missoula: got a job with a family advocacy organization, found the best hikes nearby, started writing short stories, and applied myself to breaking out of the old cycles of conflict with Mona.

Meanwhile, Louis had flown out to New York to spend his birthday—which he shared with Serala—but really to help her stay afloat in the bad season, a season bound to be worse than any before what with Jack freshly dead. Serala and Louis's love pleasantly puzzled me. There weren't characters more different on the surface. Louis was a blessing of humor and levity to everyone in his life, an easy presence, honest and discursive when need be, but definitely agreeable—versus Serala's coarseness, her eagerness to confront and disagree, her appearance of cold and closed. On the other hand, Louis and Serala both loved more profoundly and consistently than anyone I knew, besides perhaps my father. In their respective manners, they both caught loved ones in freefall—all the time. And the ease with which they helped carry others through their rough chapters demonstrated the essence of it, which Serala once said clearly to me: *Love isn't hard—it's the easiest, most natural thing in the world.* And for them it was.

Louis brought Serala medicinal laughter and lightness; he could make her giggle just by slapping on one in a repertoire of goofy faces, or sharing dark humor with her. And Serala offered Louis the inverse, the gift of severity—because of his nature, both as a dependable joker and as everybody else's confidant, Louis sometimes lacked for someone to take apart his own hurt, to remind him to do what was right for himself. And Serala could do that for all of us. Severely.

On Thanksgiving, en route to a party deep in Brooklyn, Louis, Luke, and Serala climb out of a subway station. The night is the absolute dark of autumn. By the time Louis and Luke come out of a bodega with brown bags, Serala is half a block away, fading to nothing with a large man at her side. They catch up halfway before she warns them away with a backhand like a couple of flies.

Don't fuck things up! she hollers, vanishing down a side street. They wait, painfully conflicted, until she emerges, one mission complete, dedicated to the next.

At the party, where she knows no one, she snatches a plate from the dish rack and marches to a tiny bathroom with it. Luke forces his way in with her just in time to watch her blow a whole bag of black powder off the plate with her thin nostril, five fat ridges, without even testing it.

In the days that followed, Louis spent much time alone in her living room, facing her closed bedroom door, entertaining himself with her vast CD and wine collection. He was conflicted time and again and I imagine he stood at her door indecisively more than once, even raised his hand to knock—sometimes he did. And he'd find her supine, as she'd been for countless hours, getting up only to replenish her system with the ten bags she'd bought. That white curtain would flap with winter's debut gusts, and she'd shiver, and say sweet things to him once the ease was in her veins.

He tells me about the scary drive to the big Thanksgiving bash at her folks' place, which also stands in for her birthday party. After a couple of days in bed with heroin, the turnpikes are an ominous challenge for Serala's motor skills. I can see her—because I'd taken such rides with her—stomping the accelerator casually, racing to over ninety and then dropping off again as she struggles to light a Pall Mall, until she's under the speed limit and getting honked at. She responds with a finger, which distracts her so she floats into the other lane and gets honked at again, which sets her cursing, *Yeah, yeah I see you, you fuckhead.* Louis is white-knuckled and pale, not demanding to drive because he doesn't want to hurt her pride, praying that her pride doesn't kill him. The sprawling city is soon behind and there's more room on the road, and she finds the CD she wants, and she smiles sleepily because there she is, driving, smoking, music and an old friend at her side, the best she ever could ask for—that and the tar that's in her veins.

I can see poor Louis at her elbow, walking into that house with her swaying a little, hours late for the meal. I can feel the knives in Louis's back, the dozens of stares from respectable Indians, sure that he must be the reason for their tardiness—and the sorry shape Serala is in. I can't imagine what they chalk it up to; it doesn't look much like hangover. She is a waif and her smiles are goofy, absent sort of things where they used to be bright. And the way she throws her weight around is a far cry from the tight and reserved way she ordinarily moves. I can see her walking up to a cousin, a hug and an exclamation in Gujarati, careless tug of war with the dog in the kitchen amid precarious dishes. Louis just eats and smiles in a corner, thanks her mother profusely, and tries to look as unconcerned as the rest with her grinning zombie walk and talk. He says to me, *I don't know, man, she really did seem happy.*

And I knew why, knew it wasn't just good junk, because that wasn't ever enough before. I knew why, just kept it unarticulated in my heart.

When she first calls me all fucked up on that high-grade shit she is stretching her days with, incoherently rambling, I know she's on an edge. I'm hunched before my computer in the spare bedroom in frigid Missoula, working over a short story. I can hear the TV wonk in the bedroom and Mona's trained laughter. For maybe the first time, I'm not glad to hear Serala's voice. I know the score—I've even been keeping track of how fast she could use up everything she copped at Thanksgiving.

I'm comin' to Seattle, you know, for Christmas and the fucking new year, she slurs. I get up and close the door carefully, knowing that Mona is lurking.

That's fantastic. I mean it. It's a plan! She's come up with it—I take this as very positive.

Are you going to have sex with me in Seattle?

I answer this with a dismayed silence; it's not just that the subject matter is out of bounds, it also cheapens the prior news, lumps it with the smack-fueled toss offs that will soon become common.

Are you gonna? I hear a Pall Mall ignite. She can't be that fucked up if she can still light cigarettes. *It's always so nice, you know, Eli, so sweet with you . . . like makin' love and fuckin' all at once.*

Hey, look, that's not fair. You know that's not fair. I'm out here giving it my all with Mona and you're supposed to support me.

It seems she doesn't even hear. She's just the talker now. Rambling on.

Jack's fuckin' dead. Lucky bastard.

I want to say, *No, you idiot, he's not lucky, he wanted to live. Now you have to live for him.* But I don't. I let her go on a while before I make some vague excuse to get off the line, drop the cordless, and sigh. Watch Montana's version of the moon rise in the big sky.

DAYS LATER, I'M WORN DOWN from a long afternoon of standing outside food banks, trying to get hungry, cold people to sign petitions. I'd gone to kung fu class and been thrown around by my superiors. I have only the television and Mona bathing in its light to look forward to at home. So I stop at the grocery store, to postpone my return and to grab some staple goods. As the automatic door bites closed behind me, my cell rings. I almost don't answer when I see it's her.

Hi.

Hey, love, Serala says and in those two words there is already all of it: the slur and drag of drug, but also a small tone of sheepish apology. A little brightness, as if she is excited just to rap with her best friend. I grab a shopping basket. *Where you at?*

A grocery store, surrounded by the whitest people in America, I say and she chuckles, a bright strand of sound, maybe a bit out of proportion to the joke.

Ooh, speaking of food—whatcha want me to cook for you boys over Christmas? Hold on, hold on . . . I can hear the rustle of paper and then something heavy hits the floor and a curse. But she's back on the line after a minute. *I've got a recipe for rack of lamb, raspberry truffles, pork tenderloin . . .*

I don't eat swine.

Jesus, that's asinine. I can cook a mean pig, you know.

You are a mean pig, you know, I say and gain another strand of laughter.

Guess that makes me a cannibal, she says with drugged-out thoughtfulness. *Maybe I am. Haven't you ever looked at a baby's forearms and thought, yummmmm.*

I give her a perfunctory laugh. She's been talking about eating babies for years. The line is silent for too long. I poke through a stack of frozen pizza.

Hey, yo! You there?

There's a scrambled sound, fabric pulled over the phone maybe.

You know, Eli, I'm so high. Nice and high.

Wonderful, I say flatly and move on to the bread aisle. *When do you get in to Seattle? I've got plans to make and two mean mountain passes to cross.*

The line goes dead. I listen to the buzz for a moment, then call back. I get her voice mail immediately. I select a loaf of country potato and head for the checkout.

Two nights later, with a bottle of Shiraz and Kaya at my side, with old Beatles playing on the box, I feel emboldened and serene and without much forethought I write the sentence and click the mouse and send it, buried in the context of other shit, like so much between us: *I think you need to understand that I'm not afraid of you dying.*

That this comment hits her inbox while she lies in a hospital
bed does not surprise me. She hasn't called in two days or
responded to my emails. Finally she calls and tells me (though
she hasn't told anyone else) what she ingested: three bags of
the Thanksgiving junk, triple the lethal doses of Valium and
phenobarbital, and two bottles of wine. I say:

Jeez, you'd think that'd do it.

And she says, *Yeah, you sure would.*

She'd put enough food out for Knox for two and a half days—
how long she knew it would be before her mother would come.
She'd researched the lethal dose of all three drugs and tripled it.
And again she does not die. And again she does not fall asleep.
This time, a neighbor hears her hallucinatory screams, her skull
cracking a kitchen tile.

She tells me all this in a whisper because the docs and her
folks and the shrink that she loves, even, don't know it all. She's
watching *Rocky II* from her hospital bed and she's enjoying it.

A great fucking movie, she says to me before we hang up, her
pledging to still make it to Seattle. *Just gotta get my liver working
again—gonna need it for the fuckin' holidays.*

See, I say to myself, tossing the cordless onto the bed, *I don't
feel a thing. I have peace.*

I LIKED MISSOULA; I DID well there. I got in shape; I had
beautiful hikes within a ten-minute drive. I had little watering
holes with tons of character like the Union Club. I had a beach
cruiser bicycle to take me everywhere. I had the dogs to run
with through the leash free parks. I wrote lots and lots of decent,
creepy fiction. I found great short-term jobs. But it wasn't

enough to mask the wretchedness of me and Mona.

It's a Sunday morning, bright in that way that only winter and Montana sky can be, and we're walking the dogs. Somewhere along the banks of the Clark Fork, we've managed to mire ourselves again into an argument about the future. She's badgering me about giving notice to Louis that he'll have to move out of my father's house in a year and a half—when she finishes grad school and we move back to Seattle together. I look up at the Big Sky and feel trapped anyway. I can barely breathe.

At that moment a stick-thin black lab with mange and wounds on his face trots around the corner. Our dogs bark furiously, but Mona soon coaxes him over. He wears no collar, no tags. She uses her purse strap to leash him into our pack and we continue on. She must have that whip-smart intuition working while I am silent, because she suddenly says:

If you can't commit to the future with me right now, then you should leave. I'm almost thirty-one years old and I'm tired of fucking around. So, please, do the kindest thing and leave if you can't commit to forever now.

But she didn't think I'd go. I didn't either, actually. But something final had broken.

Serala wasn't there to box up my books and slide all my papers and photos into envelopes. She couldn't keep Mona at a safe distance or wipe away my tears. But I would not have made it out that door if I hadn't known that soon—days, in fact, so soon that it didn't make any sense to drive to New York—I would be in Seattle in Serala's arms and she would make me feel right, and sane.

In twenty minutes I was lurching out of the driveway in my haphazardly stuffed truck. I cast one last glance back at the door, where Mona stood in disbelief, and then roared off behind hysterical tears into the cold sunlight, plotting wildly where to go and what to do with my wrecked self, knowing that after four years of limbo and drama and a deeply flawed love, this was the end.

I stayed on the road for a spell, carving highway circles in Oregon. Serala and I finally spoke, late on a Thursday night while Pacific waves hissed and exploded outside my window and Kaya lay next to me in the motel bed. Serala was home, back at the scene of her latest crime. Despite her damaged liver, the proximity of her latest attempt at death, her voice was like a long pull of good bourbon to me. I knew that the holidays would be not only bearable this year, but a fucking blast.

And God, we needed it.

Twenty-Two

WHEN I PICK SERALA UP at Sea-Tac, it is an odd December day: sunny and not particularly cold. And there she is, all smiles and bubbling over with excitement. I have felt this coming; I've deduced that she, like me, is absolutely determined to make these holidays sing, to mute all grief and heartbreak. She with her bag full of gifts, with her little envelope of fancy recipes, like the spirit of fucking Christmas itself. Joyous almost.

We have two hours to kill before Luke flies in, so we go to a horrendous mall near the airport to get a jump on the shopping but we end up just sitting at the cheesy Rainforest Café with the recorded hollering of monkeys, birds, and tigers leaking out of hidden speakers. Serala orders two mai tais at once.

After we pick Luke up, I can see his face in the rearview mirror as she chatters on and on to him about all our plans. I can see him enjoying the surprise he feels at her state and he says, *Yes, cool, okay, that's great,* to everything: to buying a load of booze, to shopping downtown, to cooking racks of lamb, to getting dressed up and crashing fancy lounges, to watching old movies and smoking grass.

Somewhat like my memory of our night in Memphis, the sweetness of those days sticks in me still. But the blur is close to opaque because she handed out Valiums like hard candy, even as the beer and booze flowed, as if she wanted us loose—or wanted us able to later forget.

I remember, the first night: the dusk is rising, *Harvest Moon* is wailing on the stereo, and everyone already has a cocktail. In the sky the moon is a crescent apricot.

My favorite, she says out on the porch beneath it. *A fingernail moon.* She reaches into her pocket for cigarettes, and comes out with the silver cigarette holder and silver pillbox. She snaps the pillbox open.

Oh, here, she says, and pushes two blue tablets over to me on the railing. I look at them for a moment and half a dozen good reasons not to take them flash through my mind. But then I look at her profile, silhouetted by moonlight, leaking plumes of smoke against it. I want something so badly in that moment. Not exactly to possess her, and not to save her—just maybe to be right there next to her, as close as I can be. I suppose you could say I want to keep up (which is laughable by any measure), want to inhabit the same space as her, to make it clear and loud to her that she is not alone. I throw my head back and swallow the pills with my eyes on that fingernail moon.

The cosmopolitans, and the wine, and the pills created a massive, distorted, Neil Young–sung whorl in the center of our lives. It spun us in and out as it pleased. We gave ourselves over to the mania she'd brought so fully that we didn't even question what was at its root.

I remember lurching out of a German bar and singing in the

streets, under the crescent moon, all of us—Luke, Serala, Louis, and me—clutching fancy beer steins we have none too stealthily stolen. We walk the blocks to my home with arms around each other and the mood strong and high: in defiance of all past pain and the holiday blues, we will have fun.

Weathered from broken-family pre-holidays and the pain of his brother's absence, Hugh appears on December 22. Weary, in rumpled clothes, as he comes through the door his face relights. He grins his child's grin and tumbles into Serala's arms.

We crisscross the city in my truck, all packed into the cab, wandering Northgate Mall amid the frenzy of last-minute shoppers, laughing, high on a cocktail or two, a pill, strong grass, but mainly the moment. We get confused and lost from each other and have long, funny negotiations by cell phone about where to meet. Serala finds gifts for my mom and stepfather, her with an eagle eye, closing in on the right present time and again while us boys space out and walk around aimlessly eating free chocolates offered by high school girls dressed like elves.

Then December twenty-third, twenty-fourth, and Christmas day, the three mixed up like a train wreck, and all I have left is this clutch of moments and images:

Serala drunk and smiling, tottering on high heels with raspberry truffles on a cookie tray, pleased with herself. The meal begins with a rack of lamb; the rib cage arches up out of the pan grotesquely, and we pretend to be disgusted, just to push her buttons.

God, c'mon you guys, what are you, fucking pussies? It's just a bone, she says, snapping off a section to chew on.

She's making comments about needing to score, so we drive to

Capitol Hill for dinner, just she and I, and I tell myself I'll decide my heroin policy over the meal. We sit in the back reaches of the Broadway Grill, sharing the table with shadows and the bleed of neon lights. Her eyes are a bit wild behind her green contacts, but she still smiles a lot.

Let me have a rare cheeseburger, still moving if possible, she tells the flamboyant waiter who looks at her like she's a freak. I eagerly take this as confirmation that she's okay—if she'd been feeling worse, it would have been only soda or booze. She mines the rawest of the meat out of the dish and eats most of it, then spends the rest of the meal chatting on and on about Hugh, Luke, and Louis, what glorious people they are. How Louis is *like the best kind of pot on the best of nights,* she says, how Hugh is *weary and steady, a tough old soul,* she says, how Luke is *just such a kick, the little shithead brother I never got to have,* she says.

I'm really fortunate, you know, she says, eyes lowered in some kind of humility, *to have all you guys. You can't imagine what a New England holiday would have been like. Thank you.*

I shrug this off, but her warmth has me loving, trusting, wanting to make it easier still, wanting to spoil her with comfort and love. Over the check—which she snatches and pays with her usual ferocity—I tell her I'll wait on her if she knows how to score around here, but I don't want her going far on her own. But now she shakes her head, as if at something unpleasant.

No, it's okay, the pills and you guys are enough.

But back at home she vanishes for long minutes into the bathroom and comes out unsteady, eyes dumbed and drooping, the lie of "clean" echoing in my head because she's never needed to lie before. And I know she's deep back in the muck if she's worried about scoring before she's even run out.

In other moments she is like a kid, jumping around by the little plastic Christmas tree, doling out presents, trying to get us to open them a day early. I find her sound asleep at midday on the twenty-fourth, hair wet and towel wrapped tight, beautiful in her rest, tears coming to my eyes at the sight. On Christmas morning she grins, and laughs, and rips at wrapping paper, scraps of it flying and floating on the smoky air, Beatles' guitar banging. Late that night, in the glass and steel of Seattle's financial district, she takes one of my arms and one of Luke's, walking through empty streets under a drizzle, dressed to the teeth, haunting the only bars open—five-star hotel lounges. We throw back martinis and cosmopolitans with toasts to Jack, to Sky, to my father, laughing till my face hurts at I know not what.

And, Christmas Eve, with Luke and Hugh sleepy in the light of a kung-fu film in the living room, she and I give only a nominal attempt at lying together chastely. Quickly we give our bodies over to the same voltage that joined us so many years ago in this same bedroom, the sex still like she said—*like fucking and making love at the same time*. Only now it is more tender, now with permission to hold her close even after our muscles lock, and spines arch, and breath comes like water, in gulps—even in that most fragile moment after, when she'd always had to pull a little bit away.

And I know that through all of this she was finding time. Time to get high, time to check in with her mother and the shrink, and time to do one more favor for me: call Mona and try to make her understand that this separation was real, that it was over, and that she had to go through the agony of it alone. To make her stop calling, and writing, and trying to drag me back across the mountains and into a mold I did not fit.

AT ABOUT MIDDAY ON THE twenty-sixth, Hugh comes back from his pop's place and Luke and I have more shopping to do. Serala is bent on scoring. She isn't asking me anymore, just making mention of her errand, nervous now, running low on whatever she's brought. She's grouchy, too, for the first time. She's bitching about having lost her belt and needles, asking who's hidden them. Neither losing her works nor mentioning it is like her. The elation of the days is draining out of her as the morning goes on. She paces a lot and packs and repacks her suitcase and sleeping bag mindlessly. She steps out for smokes and squints at the skyline and finally I just scribble bus directions to Capitol Hill and drop them in her lap. Having lived in Seattle herself, she probably doesn't need this, but it's a way for me to pretend at some kind of control.

I just don't want you going downtown at night, okay? I say.

I can run my own fucking errand, she says, and brushes the paper off her lap.

Luke and I split, then, me cursing a tempest about her all the way across town, laying all of the frustration and worry on his ears, him listening and nodding and finally telling me:

I found her works last night. She has been desperate at moments, merely annoyed at others, sure that someone is fucking with her. *Yeah, they were all bloody and sitting right on the bathroom counter. The problem is I don't remember what I did with them,* he tells me, rubbing his head in hungover regret. He's conflicted, of course, because he's not any more sure than I am that it's more responsible to meddle with Serala's fix than to help her find one. At the time,

I'm simply glad that he's given her a twist.

But over the hours, as always seems to be the case, my anger leaves me and I feel a tug just to get back: back to her, back to the wondrous mania, back to eulogy-in-motion, back to the music, and drink, and the love. We find a gift for her at a sporting goods store—battery heated socks for the mountains—and hurry home. Hugh is ponderous and worn-out on the sofa, as if he's been through something important but harrowing, thinning hair wild on his skull and a sheen of sweat on his brow, eyes on the unlikely sun pushing through the dead trees outside the windows. And then I get a guess as to the reason for his state, as Serala comes out of the shower, barely adequate towel wrapped around her torso. Her hair glistens and her eyes find mine and, like I am meeting her for the first time, my heart skips a beat at the heft of that glance. I follow her into the big closet and shut the door.

I'm sorry I bailed out, I say.

She puts her skinny arms around me and pulls herself close.

It's alright, she says in my ear, her face warm and pliant from the shower, against my neck. *You're allowed.*

THAT'S THE NIGHT.

Louis is playing a blues show at an Irish bar on Capitol Hill with an old bandmate. The bar is crowded with strangers as well as blasts-from-the-past for me. I say I'm going to the bar.

Get me a triple Jack, Serala says, holding up three fingers.

When Louis and his bandmate start up the thumping blues, we all migrate to the front of the crowd. The music is funky and sweet. It brings the place to life: no overdone, weepy ballads of heartbreak, just up-tempo funk and rhythm. I manage to get down a few beers in that short period, and by the time Louis is available for me to slap on the back, I find the world a bit off-kilter.

And then Serala comes to me and says, *Listen, I need to go to Second and Pike.*

The dark heart of the neighborhood where I've asked her not to go to, especially at night. This decision is the most unwelcome of any scenario. I tell her I'm in no shape to drive and I don't want her to go. But I am yielding, I am not angry, I am not pleading. I am kind, and clear, and she tells me it's fine, that she'll go in a cab.

When the taxi pulls up, I walk out with her and give her a key to my house. I say to be careful, and she says she will, and that she will see me at home. I kiss her and, before she turns and climbs into that car, she looks into my face, green contacts catching the vapor lights, and, for a long moment, she just smiles.

LATER THAT NIGHT, ON THE way to Louis's car, my phone buzzes.

Hey, love, she says. In the background I can hear several voices, casual tones, spiked by a chuckle or two: ordinary indoor conversation. *I just wanted to tell you that everything's cool and not to worry. I love you and I'll see you at home.*

I AWAKE AT 8 A.M. with Luke leaning over me.

Hey, bro, she's still not here. I grunt at him. *When can I start calling hospitals and shit?*

I tell him to wait; I feel anger turn its ugly face up inside of me.

At ten I wake with Luke leaning over me again, but this time he doesn't ask.

I'm going to start calling hospitals.

I eat my granola; I do my push-ups; I stretch and go jogging. The morning once again is golden and dappled, so odd for the season, and as I push myself hard up the muddy inclines of Ravenna Park, I pretend I'm yelling at Serala, that the pain of my lungs swelling is me giving her a piece of my mind. But I'm not worrying yet; I'm not allowing that option. She isn't going to get me all bent out of shape that easy.

Luke and Hugh leave in my truck to check in person at a few hospitals where getting info over the phone has hit a snag. When they return Luke is again sitting in our dead father's wheeled desk chair, two telephones and Serala's laptop in front of him, stepping into the role of rational leader. I watch him for a few minutes from behind as he swivels, scribbling on Post-its, opening files on Serala's computer and his own, scratching his head, blowing out sighs. The end of the sun is coming in shafts through the window above the desk. Every few seconds he falls to stillness only to jerk upright again, open another file, google something else, another idea born. My little brother—but in that moment I see him only as the man he's grown into and, simultaneously, the question of what I would do without him slams into me like a fist and with caught breath I walk over, put my hands on his shoulders.

Hey, bro, I . . . I can't break then, but I'm threatened with it so I stop, swallow, set my jaw. *Thanks for being so fucking brave.*

Luke's surprise at this caliber of compliment from his asshole older brother swells in his gaze for a moment. But then he waves it off, hugging me quick, telling me to go shower, he's got some ideas to pursue. He calls the police and they send an officer. Then he starts calling private investigators.

I dump every illegal item in the apartment into pillowcases and take them to the basement, then carefully empty Serala's bag and search every cranny, assuming, in my naïveté, that the cops will at least root through it. But the serious, by-the-book lady officer barely glances at her photo. She explains that we can file a report, but it won't do any good except to identify Serala if she turns up in a hospital—or elsewhere. She tells us with tight lips that the police never look for a missing person actively unless they are a danger to themselves or others—and hunting heroin doesn't count. We slog through the paperwork and she softens toward the end, smiles sadly once—I imagine at her impotence as much as our fear—and wishes us well.

When dark falls Luke, Hugh, and I choke down some food, gather all the information that we have, excavate old hunting knives and lengths of iron pipe from the basement, withdraw a lot of cash, and drive downtown with short breath in our breasts.

The private investigator is in Belltown, only a few grimy blocks from where the taxi took Serala. The PI is kind and competent; she takes our cash and Serala's picture and excuses herself to get to work. Idle and sliding evermore toward panic, we put up our hoods and hit the street, heading for Second and Pike.

At that intersection a diner looks out on all the shady happenings. The bar is packed with worse-for-wear characters and an occasional scary one. The waitress is plump, and weathered, and tough, and she sets down our Bud Lights, wipes her hands, and takes a look at the photo. After a minute she starts shaking her head.

Honey, I get so many people through here, I can't say. I know hundreds of faces 'cause I got hundreds of regulars, but I don't know her.

We turn back to the hookers and dealers, the drunks and addicts, all milling around one another. Certain currents peel off a duo or trio here and there, carrying them into an alley, like a great group dance on the hard, cold stage of Seattle winter. I step out to call my mom, who's been slightly panicking since she heard from Luke about the scenario. While I hunch on the leeward side of a trashcan, a black woman with an expectant or excited look on her face hurries past and I see her, through the window, appear next to Luke and Hugh in the diner. I end the call and go in. The woman is tapping her press-on nail against the gloss of the photo—*snick, snick, snick*—and exclaiming.

I know this girl! I seen this girl! Last night I seen this girl, I swear I did! I seen her up on Capitol Hill like real late last night. She was with two ugly white dudes, one of them with a big ol' steel thing through his nose—he was kind of touching her pockets as they walked and they was walking fast.

We're trying to keep our poker faces because none of us are suckers; we've all grown and wizened in this city and we know Oscar-worthy performances can leap from the minds of desperate people. This woman is moved now, though, telling us through tears that her sister is missing, too, and she'll do anything she can to help us, and do we have a phone number, and she's going right away to see if anyone knows, and we just need to pray to God Almighty and wait. Luke hands her fifteen bucks, a photo, and his number. We enter the slummy streets.

So Luke talks to dealers leaning on building facades; we find a security guard on a bike and he accepts a copy of the photo; we march dark blocks, shying away from the groups of crackheads, stopping random people and cops. We go to police precincts and drop off photos, since the police have no internal system for even circulating a picture of a missing girl. We drive to halfway houses and down notorious smack streets, passing the photo around, gripping the weapons under our jackets, leaving the phone number, floating suggestions of rewards.

Finally, I've got to call her parents. I suck down a cigarette in three drags and dial them while standing outside, in the penumbra of a cop shop. They are both on the line instantly, the terror in the back of their throats already cracking words, and I tell them very carefully everything we've done and are doing; I tell them that I let Serala go last night to score; I do my best to be honest but reassuring. We give them the PI's number, the case number, our apologies, our love. They react with the strained serenity that they have learned over the years, through a series of accidents and emergencies: concern is immediately appropriate—concern is always appropriate—but, like me, they will not allow her to yet panic them. In sober voices, they tell us to keep them posted and that their suitcases will be packed by the front door.

We go back to the Irish bar, to the last place we saw her, and it breaks me as I step over that curb. I go to the restroom to pull myself together. What knots itself in my gut is not just fear, guilt, and anger, but also disbelief, deep regret. I look at my eyes in the greasy mirror over the urinal: to think that I believed myself ready, impervious, accepting. To think that I had peace.

Then Luke gets a call from the black woman from downtown; she's in the Central District, she says, not a mile from where we are and she knows where Serala is—her boyfriend has seen her. We run to the truck and I push it hard through its gears up the steep, slick streets and thickening fog, all of us saying to one another, *This is probably a setup, let's not be suckers, we won't split up, won't follow them anywhere.*

We pull up to a gas station at the crown of the hill, big billows of fog blowing up and over like rivers of smoke. The woman stands in the yellow wash of a streetlight; her man—six-foot-something with faded clothes and a plastic bag—stands beside her. I'm not sure what happens to me in that moment, but I snap—I am absolutely done with fucking around. I pull up close with a shriek of brakes and find myself leaping down from the truck and marching up to them like I'm going straight for the jugular and they're shocked at this, move back a little and Luke and Hugh are out now, too, we're on three sides out of four and I'm saying:

What the fuck is this where the fuck is she I'm not a sucker you fucking know that?

And the tall man's eyes fly to a red Jeep Cherokee. Someone behind the tinted windows cuts it on and it rumbles away and we can tell by silhouette that there's a carload of cats in there and the tall man is whistling after them, but they've seen we're not the victims they were promised. They fishtail left out of the lot and get eaten by the ghetto's shadow. And the tall man is saying:

Well, you gonna have to come with us if you want to see her, my lady here'll stay in the car with y'all while I go up and make sure she's there, it's just down the block—

and it comes down like a guillotine in my mind: bullshit. And I breathe, release the knife in my pocket, step back and tell him:

Look, man, you bring her here and I'll give you five hundred dollars; bring her here and I'll give you whatever you want. But there isn't any fucking way that we're following you down some street—would you do that if you were me?

And he doesn't answer, thinks it's rhetorical, is searching his dopy mind for some other argument. But it's not rhetorical and I say again:

Would you do it if you were me, man?

And he shrugs, and I tell him I thought not, so go get her or stop wasting our fucking time. The woman makes her play then, coming forward with a carefully fixed steadiness in her eyes, the look of someone who has decided they are going to do wrong and do it fully—no half-stepping mumbled lies for her, no, not like her man.

You know that your girl is down there fucking smoking crack!? You know that shit? You want her down there in some fucking crack house? Do you fucking care about her? Do you love her?

She comes nearer with each phrase and she's done it now, she's convinced herself of her own theater. She's putting force into it, putting behind her words the craving of whatever it is that the reward—the bounty—would get her. And never in my life have I been closer to striking a woman. And the long moment that I spent at the house standing indecisive over the .45 pistol roars back to me. And I suck air through my teeth, and one of us tells them:

Go get her. If you know where she is, go get her. We'll be right fucking here and you can come back and get rich.

They make sounds of doubt, and shrug, and say, *Okay, we'll try,* and the man shifts the bag to his other hand and they stroll off into the fog.

Hugh says, *I'm gonna follow them, stay here,* and he pulls up his hood, and pulls down his hat, and shrugs the jacket up around his shoulders and he goes. I can't stand there, though, and I tell Luke to stay under the light and I wheel out of the station and through the lightless blocks, devouring all the black with my high-beams, making U-turns in intersections to throw light 360 degrees and there's nothing but a crackhead or two scurrying and I drive back. Hugh is there and he says, *Yeah, they just wandered off,* and we light cigarettes and haul ass to meet Louis and re-plan because the night has only begun.

At Kinko's on Forty-fifth, Luke is refining the missing person poster he's put together with the eager-to-help computer geek on the graveyard shift. Me, Hugh, and Louis are sitting on the curb and I can feel tears come and go from my vision like the tide but I won't break, can't break then, and my friends know it, even gentle Louis, and they put their hands on my shoulders, squeeze, and shake resolve into me. With a glossy stack of posters—the picture cropped from one of Serala and me on her mother's couch, both of us smiling halfway—we hit a basement bar and give a stack to one of Luke's friends who will do University Avenue. And then, toting staple guns and tape, posters and knives, we go: up and over Broadway and Capitol Hill, back yet again to the Irish bar; downtown up Third and Fourth, down Virginia and Pike. Louis drives slowly behind while the three of us move up both sides of the street, wrapping every pole with her face, pinning it onto every wooden wall, slipping it under the doors of businesses, of the needle exchange, of porno theaters. When we stop and look back down the rain-glimmering roll of Third Avenue, the streetlights wink on the gloss of her face, as if someone scattered stars down the street.

In bus stops, unhappy clots of drunks and graveyard shift workers huddle, awaiting off-hour shuttles. They watch us work, some impassive like they've seen a quartet of men do this every night, and others transfixed, watching Serala's gaze go up like the dawn to haunt them from all sides. If there is recognition in any of them, there is also a veil.

AT HOME AROUND 3 A.M. we gather on the floor, her sleeping bag threaded around us, Dad's shrine sparkling with candles, and we put on one of her mixes and take turns looking in one another's eyes and saying, *It's going to be okay, however it turns out.* I'm left to face that lie inside my own head because it belongs only there, not on the slumping shoulders of my brothers: how could it be okay if she has to keep on living now? How could it be okay if she doesn't? However it turns out, nothing is going to be okay. But her music is throbbing around us and I focus on that, try to let it lead me to some approximation of sleep.

WITH THE DAWN COMES AN end to winter's hiatus. It is cold and the rain is in earnest—Seattle at its loathsome best. The dread of facing the day, I think, gives me a taste of how she lives. How the only thing you want to do is crawl back under the covers and vanish, drive your car into the ocean. To simply go to sleep, for God's sake, and never have to rise. But there are things that have to be done.

After calling all the hospitals, the morgue, and the investigator with no results, Luke, Hugh, and I climb back into my truck. We go to saturate University Avenue more thoroughly, partly because rain has already taken some posters to the ground and mostly because we don't know what else to do. We are a spectacle of misery, inching down that busy street, jumping out like deliverymen to tack Serala's gorgeous face in every business that will allow it. We give copies to street musicians and street kids, slap it on trashcans and windows. When a man at his gyro counter refuses to put up the poster, flipping it back at me like it's my change, I come as close as I did the night before to violence and I know I need to get off the street. I find Luke and Hugh huddled outside our rendezvous, a coffee shop, Luke sucking on a raspberry smoothie in lieu of real food.

As the weepy sky intensifies its deluge, drops the size of dimes now smacking our skulls, we decide we need to laminate the posters. Just as we're about to reach Kinko's, though, Luke's cell rings and I brake in the middle of the street. I stop to hope and stop to dread. I stop to find out what it is that comes next.

Twenty-Three

LUKE TELLS US TO GET out and we do. He's on the phone, and shaking his head, and marching back and forth and then he stops: pallor floods his face, like someone pulled the drain on all his blood, and he turns the receiver away from his mouth, and breathes once and says she's been found dead in an alley downtown.

I want her closer now. I want her to look closer, to not flinch, to picture this:

Hugh is crouching under the eave of a garage, rain overflowing the gutters above him so it's like he's behind a waterfall. But I can see that he is weeping, with the stoicism that is his alone, hat pulled low, just letting the tears leak out with no expression, eyes on the winter skyline, now and then using the cuff of his coat to stab at his cheeks, the coat she gave him for Christmas four days ago. I haven't seen Hugh weep since '95 when his big brother quit the world.

Luke curses one time—*fuck*—and his right arm windmills up with the smoothie, comes down with all his strength plus gravity and the cup explodes with a *smack* in the middle of the street, a red starburst on the wet pavement, a flared wound in the side of the city. He's still young enough that when he cries he looks like a child, like someone you want to take into your arms and hush, or carry to the embrace of a mother, any mother, to comfort him. He's pale and shaking now, the phone call is done, and I know in that moment that this is how he looked when I had to tell him from ten thousand miles away that our father was gone. And now he's crying again with abandon like I've only seen when that one song is played, that song that Serala introduced us to, that song that ushers us through hard anniversaries, blasts a hole in the day clear through everything. But there's no music now, only the perpetual madness of rain, a perfunctory honk from the drivers tangled at the on-ramp. The high song of tires from Interstate 5.

And me? I'm back in the truck, brutalizing the steering wheel, my sobbing convulsive but empty and dry, and all it does is assure me of how long and far this pain will go, that I don't even get to the trailhead today, that I should have started two days ago, when I knew without knowing and put a lot of bravado and booze around me instead. And now I get out of the car and suck enough of the rain-cleaned air to make my voice work, and I dial her brother and speak the hardest words I can imagine, each syllable a marathon.

And *that*, as she used to say, *is that.*

Louis came home from work shaking, a pale face and eyes glassed over, sick that he'd not been with us for the arrival of this pain. After that, the night was composed of predictable elements: chugging whisky on our knees in front of photos of her; shaving our heads in some vague, monkish demonstration of mourning; blowing out all the speakers in the house with Neil Young. There was the destruction of an entire wall in the apartment with heads and fists, bruised and cut knuckles and faces, furniture flying off the balcony, getting kicked out of bars and, finally, collapsing into a plaster-, blood-, and liquor-stained four-person heap when we just couldn't go on any longer.

WE HAD A WINDOW OF days before we were due in Connecticut for the funeral. We headed for the mountains and all that blessed space to absorb our raging. It was a New Year's tradition for my family, something Serala was really looking forward to—a plan we had made. I'd told my mom not to cancel the festivities, not to scuttle the holiday for her gaggle of friends, but it was rough for us to mingle—though mostly everyone there wisely kept their distance.

When the time came for the bonfire—a shanty-sized pile, stacked and covered through the summer—we lit it with Molotov cocktails, a huge surge of rage spent in that one small motion. Eventually the flames were the size of horses, riding up into the swirl of stars. Luke had brought the remaining box of posters and we huddled on the sidelines of the party, slowly drawing an *X* through the MISSING and an RIP with magic markers beside Serala's green eyes. When midnight approached we split the posters four ways and I turned to the dozen or so people gathered there.

My best friend was found dead in an alley the other day, I said. *For all the years that I knew her and loved her, all that she wanted was to die. So I'd like to ask you for a moment of silence while we have this ceremony and then what we'd really like is a celebration, because that's what fits.*

In that moment, I felt something heavy slip into place in the middle of me. For the first time I got a shred of what I'd always thought I would feel when she went: relief and peace. I'd been so foolish, so young, so fucking wrong to think it would come immediately and naturally—to actually think I'd already done the work. But in that moment beneath those flames, I got a sip. But I also accepted how much I was going to have to suffer. *So bring it on,* I thought, *bring it on. If my grief will pay the passage for her out of this world, I want to feel every fucking last stab of it. Give me the fuel I need to stay open to the world.*

We circled the fire clockwise, scoping out gaps between logs to float the posters. The embers were a huge spill of searing heat and it was hard to get close enough. We managed to, though not without burns. One by one, stepping in enough to singe our brows, to release and back out, like a martial art or a dance. Her face whirled and slid with the air currents around that massive blaze, falling with something like grace into the pulsing white center, curling into the holy nothingness of ash, delivered through the whirling smoke to the impossible silence of the sky.

I WISH I COULD SAY that the funeral was good, an homage to her, something appropriate, something distinct. There were a lot of people there, but the majority didn't know my best friend, and I knew only a handful. Ceremony is good to hold families and communities together, I suppose—and, as with my father's death, the family must offer everyone the gift of closure. And dear God how her family did; I think they wept the least. When we pulled up and I saw her parents I started trembling. I climbed carefully out of the rental car and walked toward them—framed against a row of headstones and stark Connecticut sun. I wish I hadn't broken then, but I did. And I begged forgiveness for letting this happen on my watch and they held me, and hushed me, and even thanked me.

But it wasn't her. It wasn't her in that casket, almost as white as me, dead six days. A pathetic shell that didn't seem capable of having carried her and all her love through the shit world. And it wasn't her I saw mourned there, but an idea of her: a hardworking corporate VP who misread her prescriptions. But the strength in Luke's eyes was her, when he grabbed me by the shoulders in the middle of the cemetery and held me still, silent tears streaking his cheeks, a huge smile on his face as he promised me, over and over: *She's sleeping, bro. She's sleeping.*

ME, JAY, LOUIS, HUGH, SAMAR, Luke, and Adaline hit the highway hard, determined to honor Serala in a way that would have befit her. Samar and I slept, tangled together, most of the way back to Brooklyn, filling the truck with Springsteen. When we arrived, everyone was recharged for bitter celebration. We headed down to a Spanish restaurant in our funeral finery. Jay took the reins and turned it into an appropriate homage: pitchers of cosmopolitans and a massive, sizzling platter of different meats. He, the righteous vegetarian, even ate some—after a lot of loud hemming and hawing. I liked to imagine, and I suppose that he did, too, Serala arguing with him, calling him asinine and absurd. The hours that unfurled over that table will always be the crowning memory of her passing: love, friendship, history. The photos are all goofy and joyous, full of direct gazes, into the heart of the photographer, into the heart of the viewer—like her gaze, which will hang forever on my wall and peer out into my heart, my life, from that poster.

By the time we made it back to her pad that night, we mostly sang drunkenly through another couple of rounds and then flopped. But Adaline was more sensible with her drinking. She found herself awake three times that night, eyes snapping open, she swore, on Serala—staring herself down in the mirror, jeweled hands stroking the wrinkles out of her blouse, as if preparing to go to work—or maybe just to walk out that door for the last time when we all did. I don't doubt Adaline for a moment; those white drapes billowed wildly.

In January, not a week after her funeral, my mother invited Hugh to join her long-planned trip to the Caribbean. We started to get a flicker of excitement, started to hope that there might be something soothing on a tiny island parked out in the sapphire water. One of those things, we dared to dream, might be some good loving from the perfect island women we were constructing in our imaginations. A night before we left, this led Hugh, Louis, and I into the recently fallow topic of sex.

Shit, I said, *she was the only person I've slept with since leaving Montana.*

Louis chuckled a little nervously and started to say something then stopped. I figured it out, though, with a glance, so he went ahead.

Yeah, she's the last person I slept with, too.

We turned to Hugh and didn't have to ask. The laughter came into his eyes and then it came out of all of us: hard, and good, and bracing.

I lifted my bottle. *God bless her,* I said.

God bless her, they nodded, and we drank.

DID I HELP HER DIE? Did the way I loved her give her permission? Could I have stopped it and, if so, should I have stopped it? If I, her best friend, had ever confronted her with the clear hypothesis of the cycle: shame, self-hatred, and abuse, would it have gotten through and put her on a new path? In short: should I be haunted by the sweet kiss and broad smile she gave me that night on a rainy Seattle sidewalk on her way off to the end?

But I find I'm no longer much pained by that question since I spent four weeks in a little room in an artist's studio, looking out at a Vermont church and fields of snow and wrote this. I sat with piles of her letters, photos, hundreds of emails, her music, and a decade of memory. And although I had her generous brother to squeeze my shoulders and tell me, right to my face, *Thank you, you did it right, you loved her right,* I had to learn it for myself. I'm happy for her now. All my grief is just for me, just what I have to pay for having had the privilege of her love, and it is worth it. I'll carry this ache for the rest of my days, and I'll shed tears till I'm ancient, and I'll always be desperately lonely without her, but it will never stop being worth it. And it will never stop being worth it for Luke, excelling in his third year of medical school. For Louis, living in Barcelona, married and studying Flamenco. For Hugh, shouldering the world from his new home with his new love in Missoula, Montana. For Samar, fiercely alone and writing her own songs now in a bungalow in Connecticut. For Jay, running a record shop in the heart of old Seattle. For Monty, my colleague and friend, teaching literature and publishing novels not three miles from my home—my home: the same apartment, chock-full of ghosts and dogs and laughter and, also, my powerful Spanish wife and the powerful boy growing inside of her.

SERALA'S STORY IS COMPOSED OF the stories of the people who were so fiercely and well loved by her. This is just me and her. Our story is written.

And she came back to give me peace. A sleepless night in a Caribbean cabin less than a month after her death, me tossing and turning with the crash of each wave, tortured by questions: whether or not I told her I loved her, whether I did wrong by not fighting her more, whether a plan with me would have saved her. Wondering if her last hours were terrible. I got up and smoked her cigarettes, and lit a candle by her photo, and wrote to her. I asked her to let me know that she was free. And when I got back in bed and fell directly asleep, she did. She also told me the most important part: that we still have plenty of time.

And when I awoke at dawn, staring out into the sun-blasted, wind-ripped surf of the Caribbean, and I went and stood on that white sand shore, closed my eyes, put my arms out, and let the sound and fury of this world without her push the tears back from my eyes, I was assured and I was ready and I will not detain her or my father anymore. They need each other wherever they are and I need these hands and this heart to build something in this beat-up world.

AT THE END OF THE day she died, when we all finally collapsed on the floor, wrecked and spent, Louis had stretched out his arm in front of us and taken a picture—the last one on the roll—with her camera.

I have that picture now; I can see a piece of it right this second. It says it all: us with our puffy eyes, raw from tears and booze, half-smiles on our broken lips, peace (victory?) signs offered up with bloody fingers, resigned: *Fuck you, love. Thank you, love. Goodbye, love. Rest.*

So go, Serala, my traveling partner, my counselor, my drinking buddy, my teacher, my lover, my best friend. I can do it now. Go.

You're allowed.

Acknowledgments

MY GRATITUDE IS A DIASPORA.

To the other three of the fabulous four—KC, Travis, and Jeff—for standing clear-eyed and shoulder to shoulder as the darkness came down and for chiseling the pieces of light out of it.

To Alex for being able to embrace me through and across her. To Jessica for priceless support and brilliant editing and for knowing that I'd make it by writing. To Isaac and Carrie and Helena and Danielle and Tom and Daren and Drew for coming through with validation at uncanny moments. To Marc for steady doses of unreasonable poetic courage. To Thomas Weitz, for being a moonbeam for her—and for his generosity. To Tim for understanding how to love her. To Baron Wormser, Cristian Pineda, Rebecca Rubin, and Christopher Watkins—for drawing forth sparks all around me in the very deep black of a February at Vermont Studio Center. To Rudi for breath while avalanche was still falling, and for her bright dark eyes always watching. To Rachel for always reminding me what it's about, always extending a hand, and especially for giving me safety to weigh my intentions. To Doug Stewart for believing and fighting. To Ryan Fischer-Harbage for believing and fighting. To Michael Holmes for believing and fighting (and putting it on the line). To Sebastian, my Original Mentor. To Sarah, my literary guru for life. To Margaux for materializing in the eleventh hour with a wild cache of wisdom. To Peggy Shumaker, for Dawn Marano. To Dawn Marano for midwifing to the final, correct version of this book—it would quite literally not have happened without you. To Aynsley for not ever stutter stepping through the hot messes that we've shared. To Leyla for trusting me, anyway. To the crew at ECW: Crissy, Rachel, Erin, Emily, and Sarah, for rolling up your sleeves to put this unwieldy product into a hell of a box.

To Vermont Studio Center in Johnston, Vermont, the Writer's Center in Bethesda, Maryland, the Wisconsin Book Festival, and the Cross Pollination Reading Series at Vancouver Public Library for giving me places.

And to Lili—for sailing right the fuck into my harbor through a hell of a storm and staying for the aftermath and repairs (ongoing). For helping me save my life.